CONSEQUENCE OF LEADERSHIP

Consequence of Leadership

Principles of Leadership - Revealed from within a Large Organization

Craig Mostat

© Copyright 2009 by Craig Mostat

All rights reserved

Cover design by Bryanna Mostat

Published by Lulu.com

Scripture quotations marked (NIV) are taken from the HOLY BIBLE, NEW INTERNATIONAL VERSION®. NIV®. Copyright© 1973, 1978, 1984 by International Bible Society. Used by permission of Zondervan. All rights reserved.

Scripture quotations marked (MSG) are taken from The Message. Copyright © 1993, 1994, 1995, 1996, 2000, 2001, 2002. Used by permission of NavPress Publishing Group."

Scripture quotations marked (MKJV) are taken from the Holy Bible, Modern King James Version. Copyright © 1962 – 1998 by Jay P. Green, Sr. Used by permission of the copyright holder.

Paperback ISBN: 978-0-557-05600-2

TABLE OF CONTENTS

Preface 7

Chapter One
Unique Perspective 11

Chapter Two
Focus & Clarity 23

Chapter Three
Listening and Leading 43

Chapter Four
Customer Focused 67

Chapter Five
Don't let the "accountants" take over 87

Chapter Six
You are only as good as your weakest link 111

Chapter Seven
Simplify 127

Chapter Eight
Recognition 155

Chapter Nine
The future of Effective Leadership 169

Notes 181

PREFACE

It is early 2009 and we are in the midst of what could possibly be the worst economic downturn that the world has experienced. It seems almost every day we hear of another bank, investment corporation, company or business that is in financial trouble. These same organizations are restructuring, downsizing, laying off, seeking government bailouts and/or entering into bankruptcy protection. The media reports suggest and imply that these corporate failures are because of the economy. Not surprisingly, these reports are used to bolster the negative economic news of the day in order to sell more newspapers and keep the electronic news media as captivating as possible. A lack of knowledge and awareness is what allows these negative reports to take root in us.

When we are properly informed, we can rightly discern and understand the reports of corporate challenges and failures due to the economy, reducing the atmosphere of anxiety that exists today. The fact is that these business failures, with only few exceptions, are not the result of the current economic realities, but are actually the outcome of decisions made within those organizations, months, years and sometimes, even decades prior to the current time. These troubled corporations make up only a minuscule fraction of all the businesses, companies and organizations that exist. The reality is that the vast majority of businesses continue to operate with very little problems or turmoil despite the economy around them. Certainly some experience a softening of the results, but these temporary "blips on the radar" do not cripple and ruin them. The economic downturn has only exposed the feeble, weak and poorly operated organizations in the same way that a disease strain in a herd of animals takes the sick and weak as its victims. It is certainly easier for these troubled companies to blame the economy for their problems, but in most cases is not reality.

This is not the first recession and will not likely be the last. Businesses will continue to fail regardless of the state of the economy while at the same time others will thrive. We need to uncover the reasons behind these successes and failures.

Fortunately, we can learn from history – from the mistakes and achievements of others. We can avoid the pitfalls that have caused others to fail and can leverage good habits, practices and strategies that have been utilized by others to succeed. The outcomes that we see – both positive and negative - are the result, or consequence, of the leadership.

People who ask our advice almost never take it. Yet we should never refuse to give it, upon request, for it often helps us to see our own way more clearly.

Brendan Francis

Chapter One

UNIQUE PERSPECTIVE

I have a unique perspective. I have worked in the rank and file of a well-known Canadian retail chain for the past 24 years. Starting at the lowest levels of the company; at the bottom - the stock person pushing carts - I worked my way up through the ranks to a position in middle management, remaining at that level for six years to work and observe.

I have watched and worked with many different leadership styles and have observed many different approaches to leadership. I have seen both successful and unsuccessful programs in operations, marketing, training, planning, logistics, etc. I have been given the opportunity to experiment and test different approaches myself to see what really does work and what does not. I have lived with both the benefits and consequences of decisions made by those at the highest levels in the company.

So what makes this perspective unique? Many who have

this same view of their organization or company - the distinct ability to observe from the inside of the organization - would also have this same unique perspective. In particular, anyone else that is in the position of "middle management" or a "middle level manager".

A "middle manager" is that position between the "top managers" and the "first line managers". "Middle managers'" job titles include general manager, plant manager, regional manager, divisional manager and in my case district manager.

Existing at this level in any organization can be both the most rewarding, and the most frustrating of positions. There are two key reasons for this:

1. You are still in touch with those that are closest to the customer and;
2. You are in touch with and have an opportunity to influence those that are making the decisions.

Let me explain:

The "middle manager" is the connection between the two (customer & decision makers). Initiatives do not move forward, communication does not happen, projects do not get started without the "middle manager".

In successful organizations, those that make the decisions are still in touch with the customer. This can be through conducting and listening to customer surveys, speaking to those on the front lines, seeking input through the organization hierarchy or a combination of all the above. Decisions, when made in the best interest of the customer, are usually the right decisions. Sounds logical and makes sense – right? Unfortunately, it does not always work like this and in some companies and organizations, the chief decision makers are not in touch with the customer.

Fortunately, for the company/organization, and the customer, we have the "middle manager". He or she can step in and influence the decision makers to adjust initiatives in order to increase their effectiveness in meeting the customer's needs. Moreover, when heard, this can be the most rewarding part of the "middle manager's" work life.

On the other hand, decisions made in a vacuum without the customer's best interests in mind, alienate the customer and frustrate organizations. The "middle manager" can see, feel, taste, smell and touch this frustration. They live it everyday through their team on the front lines. If they are not heard or are not able to influence the decision-making, all of that frustration continues to live at and below the "middle manager".

This book is not about "middle managers". The explanation above is simply to illustrate the unique view that a person in this position has of a company or organization. I would argue that any "middle manager" in any organization, has the clearest view of anyone to see what is really happening, how decisions are really affecting those in the front lines and ultimately the customers. An individual in this position has first hand knowledge of the experiences and challenges of both those that directly serve the customer and those that directly serve the top of the organization. They are the go between and the balance between the two entities.

Those that hold the position of "middle manager" in any organization also carry great responsibility. If we were to compare an organization to a simple machine - "the lever": in healthy, working, vibrant companies, this position [middle manager] is the fulcrum or the support of the organization (lever). The "middle manager" is the balance and centre point. When one side (senior leadership) exerts pressure in the form of a business strategy, plan or initiative, it is entirely dependent upon the "middle manager" to make the other side (the front line) "go up" or produce from that initiative. If the position or individual is out of balance to either side, it will be difficult to make any initiative work successfully for the organization.

The principles in this book are from the perspective of one from the middle of an organization. They are based on a real company and real life experiences. The company that they are garnered from has had reasonably successful times during my tenure. However, in recent years the company has struggled to generate any real momentum. It is the last 15 years that these principles have become amazingly clear. They are a collection of what to do to bring back or kick start a struggling organization and the "what not to do" in order to avoid smothering a company's ability to succeed. At the same time, they are solid principles for any new organization to use to ensure not only survival, but also the ability to thrive.

I have also discovered that organizations are not very different from each other. Amazingly similar parallels can be found between any two organizations. Regardless of whether they are "for profit", "not for profit", private or public sector, cultural, political, etc, successful organizations generally have the same characteristics, as do unsuccessful organizations. I suspect that as you read this book you will be surprised at the comparisons that you will be able to make to your own organization, company, or personal situation.

Using the history and experience from the organization

that I worked within, I have provided specific examples of how decisions actually effect organizations, the people in them and the customers that they serve. Constructive and beneficial suggestions and principles for more effective leadership have also been provided, some of which, you will have no doubt heard before. I believe all of these [principles] are rooted in common sense and logical thinking, yet are often and unfortunately overlooked or forgotten in many organizations.

The lessons gleaned from this company and the leadership principles contained within will be of benefit to any person, in any position, in any organization. They will provide insight, knowledge and with application – wisdom, to those that hold positions at the top of any company or organization. All leaders, at any level of an organization have teams of people – their own organizations if you will - and therefore will gain the same insights and benefit from this book. In addition, these principles, once internalized, will provide clarity to anyone within the organization – from those at the lowest levels through and beyond the middle manager, and enable them to lead effectively upwards. In other words, they will be more informed and prepared to influence those in the top decision-making positions of any organization. Finally, these principles are universal. Every person on this planet is a leader in some respect. A Mother provides leadership to her children – a teacher to his/her students – a student to their peers – friends to each other. I believe that the best leaders also lead up. This means that sometimes a child can provide leadership to the parent, the student to the teacher, the front line employee to the CEO (chief executive officer). The lessons and principles contained within will help any person to become a more effective leader in any arena of their life.

You will have noticed that I have used the words organization and company interchangeably. These principles are applicable to any organization - large or small business, church or non-profit organization.

I have chosen to substitute the name "The Company" for the real name of this organization. My decision to do this is two fold. The first is that my comments and stories about "The Company" are not entirely complimentary and I do not think that "The Company" would appreciate what I have written. The second reason is that the actual name of "The Company" is not relevant - the lessons and principles are. I feel that I have more than adequately explained the problems and solutions without having to divulge the name of this organization.

While I do share a fair amount of detail about "The Company", this book is not intended to be a case study or review of "The Company". Since it is based upon the lessons learned and observed from within the organization, I felt it was necessary to provide a clear view into the inside of "The Company" to effectively demonstrate why the principles provided are so essential. The stories and examples are all in support of the leadership principles examined and reinforced. I expect that you will find the examples used provide a great amount of contrast to the principles as well as serve to underpin them. It is my objective that you will gain beneficial insight into leadership and business principles rather than what went wrong with a particular organization. However, at the same time, observing the consequences of poor leadership can also be beneficial and serve to help us avoid pitfalls.

You may find my comments, stories and situations about "The Company" particularly critical, primarily because they are. We learn best when we make mistakes and fail. "The Company" has certainly not done everything wrong. The principles and guidelines recommended throughout this book are based on both the good and the bad. However, it is often the negative experiences, mistakes, and failures that so effectively illuminate the right thing to do. It is for this reason that I have chosen to focus on them.

"THE COMPANY"

A well-established national Canadian retailer that has posted very successful results at times during its existence, but has not realized any significant success in the past 15 years. With a tall organizational structure (meaning many levels of management), combined with starkly separate functional divisions, the organization works in "silos" very separate from each other. I guess that is why they call them "divisions". The word "silo" meaning a tall cylindrical tower used for containing or storing, is a perfect metaphor to describe how the divisions of the company work in isolation from each other.

The company lacks focus on why they are truly in business and on whom the customer is that they are trying to serve. While this may not be obvious to an observer outside of the organization, if you were to ask anyone inside the organization, you would be left with little doubt. Remembering why you started and what you are in business to do is critical to success. Surprisingly, this becomes a challenge for many organizations, particularly as they grow. If you were to look behind the curtain of any struggling company, I suggest you would likely discover this issue at the root of their problems. This subject will be the focus of the second chapter.

"The Company" has seen many different leadership changes trying to find success in the Canadian marketplace. Each of these different leaders contributed to altering the culture over time. Some of this culture change has been very positive. Take for example the culture of respect that currently exists. Respect is foundational to positive relationships across, and up and down in any organization. However, respect without honesty creates an entirely new set of problems and will keep an entire organization pegged to the ground unable to move. We will discuss this further in chapter three.

"Customer focused" is the claim of the organization as it is with most in today's world. Regrettably, this is largely lip service in this particular company, which anyone outside of the organization – customers - notice with relative ease. It is not that "The Company" does not want to be customer focused. It truly does. It is just that the organization wants everyone on the front line to be "customer focused", and does not really believe that anyone else in the organization needs to be - just those that directly serve the customer. I will explain in detail what this looks like in the fourth chapter.

In pursuit of past success, this company has become proficient in measurements and metrics (buzz word for measurements). "What gets measured gets better" is the guiding philosophy, meaning and suggesting that if it is measured something will be done to improve it. Metrics provide both the benchmarks (where we want to be) and comparisons to benchmarks. Metrics let you know where you stand. But, how much measuring is too much? Where do you draw the line? I have experienced first hand what happens when a company fails to draw the line on what it will and will not measure.

In this company, unimaginable payroll dollars, time, and energy are spent on software development and spreadsheet/scorecard production. Even more alarming is the un-measurable amount of time and energy (likely the only elements not measured) that is spent just to analyze the reports and analysis that have been created. Please do not take the wrong idea about what I am saying; metrics are an important tool and most certainly have a place in achieving improved results. However, we are talking about a retail organization that has reporting and spreadsheets that would marvel any national government and amounts of data that could compete with the data collected to build and launch the space shuttle. The fifth chapter, "Don't let the 'accountants' take over", will identify the pitfalls that this can cause and where any organization should draw the line.

The old adage "You are only as good as your weakest link" is true. Any organization or team is only as good as its weakest facility, its weakest division, its weakest store etc. In retail for example, if the buying office does a poor job buying, no amount of effort on the part of the stores can make it better. Conversely, if the buying office buys a stellar line-up of product, but the stores drop the ball and fail to get the goods to the selling floor, the great buy will not realize its maximum potential. In chapter six, we will explore this in more detail and expose how one weak link can affect an entire chain. We will also discover why ignoring the issue hoping that it will go away is never the right answer.

CONSEQUENCE OF LEADERSHIP

"Never tell people how to do things. Tell them what to do and they will surprise you with their ingenuity" General George S. Patton

Some people like detailed instruction. Some do not. If you want your organization to be filled with entrepreneurial decision makers that come up with new ideas, make sound decisions and generate superior results, do not overwhelm them with instructions. Chapter 7 will outline how one organization completely and continuously *carpet-bombed* "how-to" and "instruction" that was often stating the obvious or contradictory direction.

I will explore the subject of recognition in chapter 8. The appreciation, acknowledgement and gratitude that are vital to ensure you continue to retain and stimulate those which most companies call their most important asset – their people. If companies truly understood this concept and did not only give it lip service, there would not be an absence of the recognition formerly mentioned.

In the final chapter, I will argue the destructive nature of "political correctness" and the negative consequences that this has on society in general. I will also tie together each of the principles identified and provide my view of what the most effective leader looks like and the characteristics that they demonstrate.

Make no mistake; if "The Company" does not make drastic changes to its culture, focus and operation, it will eventually fail. As I write this, in the year 2008, the downturn of the global economy and worldwide recession could be the final straw that breaks the back of "The Company" that has already experienced more than 10 years of its own economic recession. If it does not engineer and execute a major transformation in the manner that it conducts business, it will fall to the ranks of those now forgotten Canadian retailers or be purchased by some other larger company, and changed to another format entirely. When this happens many of the "analysts" will come forth and try to explain what "The Company" did or didn't do to cause their own demise, and certainly many of the mistakes will be even more obvious than they are today. However, they will not be able to explain what brought the organization to that point – why they made those mistakes. The troubles of a struggling organization are often the consequences of years, perhaps decades, of poor leadership and decision-making. This predicted outcome for "The Company" has not yet transpired, but the answers to those future questions of why and more importantly, the solutions to the problems, are both contained in the chapters of this book.

Each chapter begins with real life examples from "The Company". I will give you insight into the "inner workings" of this organization and the consequences of the actions and strategies (or lack of). The lessons and principles that have been gleaned from the operation of this company will then complete each chapter.

I encourage you to read through the journey and "learnings" from a real life experience in a Canadian company. Wisdom will speak to you as you read these principles and I believe that you will intuitively understand that they are true and worth examining in your own organization. If your organization is struggling, look at each of these areas to make a positive and lasting change.

*If you don't know where you are
going, you can never get lost.*

Herb Cohen

Chapter Two

FOCUS & CLARITY

"THE COMPANY"

As with all organizations, "The Company" started with a purpose. Relentless focus on that purpose created immense success. Then adversity hit. The adversity in this case, as it was for many retailers, was the entry of new competition into the Canadian retail marketplace. "The Company", tossed about on the new stormy seas of formidable competition, lost their identity. They failed to stay on their mission – to stick with their purpose.

Perhaps that purpose was not as clear as it needed to be in the first place. Perhaps the company was just lucky when it was successful and had the benefit of weak competition. I do not believe so. Companies do not achieve success without a clear sense of purpose, at least not for any significant amount of time.

No, this company let go of the wheel of the big ship and

allowed it to drift for many years – 15 years. Some tried to take hold of the wheel and put the ship on a course, but in each case, the new course was not clearly outlined. Due to the absence of good communication, only the person that had the wheel (the president) truly understood where the company was going, and it was often felt – due to a lack of clarity - that even they were making it [vision/purpose] up as they went along. Eventually, it became clear that they did not really have a vision, and someone with more decision making power would relieve them from the wheel, bring in a replacement and the cycle would repeat itself.

How could this continue to happen? Why would every new leader repeat the mistakes of the previous ones – charting their own course, and then fail to properly clarify and communicate it? The answer: Lack of humility and the existence of arrogance or big ego's - the "leader knows best" mentality. This created the failure to try to understand the landscape accurately before charting the course - failure to understand the problems before developing the solutions. I will delve into this much further in a subsequent chapter.

In the past 15 years (the era that the lessons in this book come from), "The Company" has had mission statements - of sorts - under various names and formats. The most unusual of these was "The president's 21 key priorities". Needless to say, the number "twenty one" does not fit well together in the same statement as the words "key" and "priorities". Never the less, "The Company" operated under this for well over a year and since it provided no real and meaningful direction – there wasn't any.

There were years with absolutely no mission whatsoever. One could ask any person in the organization to see if they could explain the mission during this time (which I did regularly) and receive an answer of bewilderment. Interestingly, asking this question would often push the "yes people" (explained later in the book) into a state of anxiety and mortification when through that questioning, they came to a realization that they were operating without any purpose or direction. It is interesting that so many can carry out "busy-work" every day, with no understanding of purpose or vision for the future, and seem to find fulfillment in the myriad of those often directionless projects and activities. However, that subject is best reserved for another book.

During the past 15 years, there has only been one mission/purpose statement out of many, which the entire organization generally understood - only one that would resonate with an outsider to the company if allowed to see (my litmus test for mission statements). This mission statement was comprised of only four words. It described who the customer was with amazing clarity - what "The Company" was there to do for that customer - how they were to do it and the "when" and "where" were easily implied and understood. People could by into it – they understood it. Not surprisingly, with this clarity of purpose the company made improvements, began a comeback and made some progress. It was under this clarity of purpose that the most positive changes were made to once again, connect with the customer. With such clarity, the future looked bright, except for one problem - focus. Reminiscent of the common housecat lured in a different direction by the most insignificant object, anything (or anyone) without a dedicated purpose can be distracted. It has been said "Curiosity killed the cat", for good reason. It was this lack of focus on that reason – the purpose - that the "The

Company" exists, which prevented it from finally getting back on to a successful, solid and continued path – and despite the fact that they had a great vision, they once again went off course.

The most vivid evidence that "The Company" failed to renew its purpose is that the customers still think – to this day – that "The Company's" mission is the same as it was 20 years ago. This is despite attempts to redefine itself multiple times. Imagine how disappointing it is for customers to come into any organization expecting one thing while the company is trying to deliver something entirely different. Imagine the frustration of both the customers and the company because of this lack of clarity, focus and communication. The power of the principles of "focus" and "clarity" is profound indeed – contributing either negatively or positively. It is important to understand that there are consequences – good or bad - to all principles depending on how they are used, ignoring them leaves the outcomes to chance.

In the days that the company was successful there was one leader - one person who ultimately oversaw the entire organization. I am not referring to a specific person, but rather a position. This leader would keep everyone in the organization focused on the mission – the purpose. This is key. It prevents empire building and development of individual agendas and this is precisely what has happened in "The Company" during the past 15 years. The hierarchy was changed to a structure that allowed multiple leaders to set the direction causing a great amount of ambiguity and confusion.

With a vacuum or lack, of strong leadership in the top position, those below began to take over. They built their empires, and began to build walls around their empires. The organization became a series of silos operating in isolation from each other. Each operating silo began to make decisions for the benefit of their silo rather than the organization as a whole. For example:

- Distribution would make decisions to cut costs that actually created several times more expense than what was saved. However, this additional expense was at store level – not in the distribution silo.

    The Result: Distributions performance looked outstanding while the stores performance decreased. Animosity grew between the divisions.

- Merchant/buying group would initiate store layouts and set-up timelines that were unmanageable and unachievable at store level.

    The Result: Stores fell behind. New lines of merchandise purchased sat in the backroom for lack of space on the floor resulting in loss of sales and increases in inventory. Fuller backrooms created backlogs, which decreased the "in-stock" on other items.

- Marketing would create advertising that replenishment was unable to supply.

    The Result: Customers were disappointed when they arrived at the store to purchase advertised products that were not available. Frustrated store associates.

This continued for years and unfortunately continues today. Once again, this problem of operating in silos is surprisingly easy to see and most inside the organization can and do see it. Amazingly, even those at the top of each Silo (VP's and Senior VP's) can also see it but have done little or nothing to change it. It is the vacuum in leadership at the top and the lack of openness and honesty in all communication that prevents any real change.

During those times when "The Company" had no clear purpose or mission, the focus moved to activities and initiatives. Without the guidance of "purpose", every initiative becomes a good idea. Every activity is worthy. How can anyone oppose? What would be the reason for opposition to a new initiative? What argument could one use to suggest that the initiative or activity does not fit with the company's strategy without a clear understanding of that strategy?

As a result, "The Company" became an activity driven machine. The implication was - the more initiatives and activities – the more imagined progress. Work harder and the results will come. Do more. Initiate more. Create more programs, systems, and procedures. More and more "Busy-work" was created. Success was defined as those who could execute the most activities – those who could juggle the best. Good thinking was all but eliminated. Eventually creativity and entrepreneurship was almost completely stifled – who would dare add another program and activity to the already overwhelming workload. The organization became filled with "do-ers" - trained and obedient managers that worked in the system, managed the system, but never questioned the system.

In the end, we have an organization, without a clear sense of purpose, filled with great people working harder and harder trying to accomplish better results, but not even clear on what those better results truly look like or when they have reached a good level. The results do not come, so everyone works harder – more activity - and then frustration sets in. Frustration leads to apathy and at the time of writing this book – this is where "The Company" exists. A visionless organization filled with apathetic hard working great individuals. Unless someone sticks their hand in the spinning wheel of this doom loop – this organization will fail and fall to the ranks of the closed and forgotten Canadian retailers.

ONE FINAL EXAMPLE – THE MOST DRAMATIC

It would seem logical that a retail company should "exist" to sell merchandise to their customers. If you were to think of any retail store, it would not be wrong to assume that they make their profit from the goods that they sell. However, "The Company" does not actually make any significant profit from their retail operation. In other words, they do not make money from the selling of merchandise. Fortunately, this company has "credit products" – a credit card. Credit is a lucrative business in any form and has been the main profit centre for this company. In fact, without the credit products that this company offers, the doors would have closed many years ago.

For this reason, the focus on maximizing credit revenues exceeds anything else. It is the number one priority of everyday life for this company. There is exponentially more emphasis on this one issue than any activity aimed at trying to sell more merchandise to customers. In fact if one were to write a mission statement in reverse based on the inner workings of this company it would read:

"To maximize Credit profit"

Now, remember this is supposed to be a retail company

and retail companies sell merchandise. In reality, they are a credit lending organization that uses retail stores to sell their credit product. I believe that there are no right or wrong mission statements, which I will explain later in the chapter. If this company were to admit that this is in fact why they exist and adopt this as their purpose – they would ultimately achieve some success, particularly compared to the results they are getting today. This, in my opinion, is the most alarming example to illustrate the lack of direction, clarity and focus of this organization.

THE PRINCIPLES OF "PURPOSE" AND "FOCUS"

Strategic planning is worthless -- unless there is first a strategic vision.
John Naisbitt:

Every worthy endeavour must have a purpose or focus - a reason for existence. This purpose is the reason that a business or organization is formed in the first place. It is the what, how, who, when and where of the organization. The "what" you do, and how you do it. The "who" you serve, "when" you serve and "where" they (customer) and you are located. The more clearly defined the purpose/mission is - the more focus and ultimate success the organization will have.

Non-profit organizations are typically more focused than those businesses that exist to make a profit. They rarely forget why they exist because they do not have the competing and alluring issue of making a profit, although raising funds to support their endeavour can sometimes become a substitute. The undeniably important issue of making a profit is not the purpose of any organization. Nor is the goal to create value for the shareholders. Certainly, these are critical to an organization's long-term success, but if an organization exists for these outcomes only, success is not likely to be obtained or sustained.

Designing your product for monetization first and people second will probably leave you with neither.
Tara Hunt, HorsePigCow

No business or organization begins with the sole purpose of making money. This idea may be the incentive to start something, but it is not the purpose. For example, if you see an opening to provide a dry cleaning service in your market, you could start your own business to take advantage of this opportunity. The incentive for you to do this would be of course to make money. However, the purpose behind the business is to meet the dry cleaning needs of your customers and the more focus and clarity that you place on this purpose - the more successful you will be.

A dry cleaner near where I live has designed their facility with a drive through. Instead of walking through the front door to drop off or pick up your laundry, one only has to drive up to a window exactly as they would at any fast food restaurant with a drive through. I go there because I would rather not get out of my car. It is convenient. It is clear that this business owner understands that he/she exists not only to meet the dry cleaning needs of the customer, but to make it as convenient as possible as well. If he/she were in business only to make a profit, it would be very unlikely that this convenience would have ever been added. Why? Adding a drive through would have added considerable costs to the construction of the building. Shortsighted thinking - only focused on profit and nothing else - would likely not have come up with an idea that would add costs.

The creativity and innovation that you see in the marketplace is not arrived at by chance – but rather by understanding why you exist, what you are trying to accomplish, and remaining focused on it.

MISSION STATEMENTS

Many organizations state their core purpose in the form of a mission, purpose or vision statement. This is typically a one sentence or one paragraph statement that outlines the five "W"s to an organization's existence. It provides the guidelines or framework in which the organization will work. It should provide the path that the organization is to move on and while not usually stated, imply the boundaries that will keep the organization on course.

This is a very simplistic explanation of the "Mission Statement", an entity that has grown to become incredibly complex. I believe that the sophistication of "Mission Statements" has deemed them generally useless and a waste of time for all. The previous paragraph is what they are intended for and when they serve this purpose, they can galvanize organizations on course. However, from my standpoint, they need to be brought back down to earth to ensure that they serve the real purpose for which they were designed.

We have too many high-sounding words, and too few actions that correspond with them.
Abigail Adams (1744 - 1818), letter to John Adams, 1774

The simpler and easier to read and understand the mission is; the more widely it will be used as the guiding purpose for an organization. If it is filled with sophisticated words and difficult to understand business axioms, few will comprehend and use it. While it may look impressive, what you really want is everyone – yes everyone - in the organization to understand and follow it, from the lowest level position to the CEO. In fact, if an outsider to the organization was to read but could not easily understand your mission statement - your purpose for existence – it would not likely be understood and followed by anyone inside your organization.

There are vast amounts of resources and people to assist you in the design, structure and writing of a mission statement and I would not claim to be an expert on this subject. However, I have had to live through many mission statements – both inspiring and foundational, as well as the vague, wordy and empty. What I mean by "live" is to try to understand, and apply them in my work and leadership. I have seen them from the frame of reference of one in the lowest levels of an organization as well as various levels of management. I can easily tell you which ones are good and will work to achieve the goals of an organization, and those that will only confuse the masses.

The following are guidelines that I would suggest be followed when developing a mission/purpose statement. Note: For the sake of clarity to those that have a more comprehensive understanding of mission statements, I am referring here to the "vision" or "purpose" component of the mission statement.

- Write it as specific as possible, but yet as universal as possible. I.e.: The mission statement "To make the best nails in the world" is very specific. "To produce the most effective and efficient building fastening products worldwide" is both specific and universal.

- Use as few words as possible – if you can write it in fours words – great. If your purpose can be stated in one word – even better. I.e.: in the example provided above, we could say, "develop and manufacture", but instead chose the word "produce". Same thing – less words.

- Use the simplest words possible. Look at each word that you have written and challenge it downwards with a thesaurus in hand. Big words do not necessarily imply intelligence. You want everyone in your organization to understand by just reading it – once.

- Never use buzzwords or phrases (organization specific slang or jargon). Buzzwords always change and they always aggravate people in the organization due to their overuse.

- Do not mention profit, shareholder or share value. I realize that my advice on this one is very controversial. However, your purpose is not about any of these. If you focus on your true purpose - the profit and shareholder value will come.

After writing your mission statement but before you adopt it, test it. Ask people in your organization at all levels if they understand what it means. Ask them how it applies to what they do and how they can apply what they do to it. Look at their feedback with honesty and ask yourself some questions.

- Do I think that this mission statement/purpose will resonate with my organization?

- Did anyone offer any opinions or advise that would cause me to amend it?

- What will this "mission statement" actually achieve for my organization? What will it get me?

If necessary, change it.

Bureaucrats write memoranda both because they appear to be busy when they are writing and because the memos, once written, immediately become proof that they were busy.
Charles Peters

Many organizations, in fact most in my opinion, write mission statements because they think they have to. Rather than writing to provide clarity of purpose, they are often written to ensure that the organization looks legitimate – as if someone once said that an organization is not authentic, valid, genuine or real until there is a mission statement in place. So the senior team disappears for a weekend, up the mountain into isolation. They come down with the stone tablets, and on them, the words of the "mission statement" have been written. Oh yes - and their faces are gleaming with the glow of enlightenment because they have now *seen* the mission. They proclaim that they now have the vision for all to follow.

There are at least two problems with this:

1. Why is an organization that has been in existence for any length of time, writing a mission statement? Either they have forgotten the original reason that they are in business, or the landscape has changed and there is a feeling of a need of change of the mission statement.

2. If an organization is writing this "mission statement" mid stream (again a major problem), why not ask those that are closest to the customer for their input? Contrary to the egotistical wisdom of some leaders, there are others in the organization that may just have some very good insight. They might actually have better answers to the questions. In fact, they may

even have better questions.

We will explore point two in much more detail in the third chapter. An organization that has lost their way, as indicated in point one - so much so - that they feel the need to "only now" write a mission statement, is in trouble indeed.

The most successful organizations on the planet all have commonalities, among which is the fact that they have never forgotten why they exist. These organizations have stayed the course. They have continuously followed the guiding philosophy of their core purpose. As a result, they have not lost focus and steered off course. They have continued to operate their organizations with amazing clarity and have obtained continuously increasing revenue and profits – in other words – success.

If you find your organization in a position that you feel you need to write a mission statement, go back to your roots. Think back to the reason that you created your business or organization in the first place. If you can recapture and restate that core purpose, you will bring back the success that your organization once realized.

Again, the mission or purpose, stated correctly, should stand the test of time. It needs to be both specific and universal. Read the attached "Mission Statements":[1]

Wal-Mart "To give ordinary folk the chance to buy the same thing as rich people"

Mary Kay Cosmetics "To give unlimited opportunity to women"

3M "To solve unsolved problems innovatively"

Merck "To preserve and improve human life"

Walt Disney "To make people happy"

Anyone outside these organizations can easily understand why these organizations exist – what their purpose is simply by reading their "Mission Statement". These are not mystifying statements, but instead both easy to understand and apply. They are actually inspirational and make it easy to buy into and rally behind with a unified "Yes". Furthermore, it is difficult to imagine anything that could cause these organizations to have to change or adapt their purpose to changing times – they are universal enough to stand the test of time.

- In the case of Wal-Mart's purpose – there has always been both rich and "ordinary folk". There always will be.
- Would there ever be a reason for not giving unlimited opportunity to women as stated in Mary Kay Cosmetic's mission statement?
- 3M understands that we will always have problems, and they will likely always be around to solve them innovatively.
- As long as we have human life we will continue to have mission statements and Merck will likely be around to help preserve it.
- People will always have a desire to be happy – that will never change. The Walt Disney Corporation will no doubt be around for a long time working to that end.

There is not a right or wrong mission statement. Your organization's purpose is whatever you deem it to be.

Certainly, it would be advantageous to make your purpose relevant in today's world. Starting a business that endeavours to manufacture the best quality wagon wheels would be difficult (but not impossible) to find success. Not impossible? The most ingenious entrepreneur could begin a thrust to bring back the horse and cart combination based on the current push for reduced carbon emission in an attempt to thwart global warming.

Regardless of what your purpose is, it must be clear. I cannot imagine any individual or leadership team sets out to make a "Mission Statement" that is written in a code only understood by a choice few. However, it happens and far too often.

Clarity inspires the organization to action. Clarity eliminates ambiguity. It is simply impossible to focus on anything that you do not understand. Clarity of purpose, keeps everyone on course – particularly in times of difficulty and challenge. If you know where you are going and are clear on the specific course that will get you there, you are less likely to be enticed by every side show and opportunity that could take you off course. There are an infinite number of great opportunities, but not every opportunity is great for everyone or every organization.

"The Company" is certainly not the only organization that struggles with "Focus" and "Clarity". I have come to understand that the vast majority of large companies and organizations suffer from this same type of wandering. With the steady lure of opportunities in all kinds of directions, it is easy to fall into the temptation of a different direction that does not fit within the framework of your company's goals. You cannot be good at everything. In fact, companies should stick to only those things that they can be the very best in.

Returning to the example of "Credit" at "The Company", discovering and capitalizing on other streams of revenue and profit is smart business. Some other obvious examples would be extended warranties, loan insurance, and after sale installation or technical services. Most, if not all of these are pure profit with very little or no cost. Because of this easy money, businesses are tempted into putting more and more time and emphasis into them. When this happens, the core of the business will begin to erode away. Organizations must maintain a sense of discipline to keep their focus on that, which is the reason they exist.

Organizations always start with a clear focus. It is because of that clarity of focus that they achieve any kind of success initially. However, for some, this success has a way of causing them to wander off the path on which they started. It is the leader that sets the direction and new leaders will often feel compelled to change that direction – make their mark, so to speak. Changing direction (the mission) is risky, but with any risk, there is a potential upside.

First, I would submit that a change from the path that brought your organization success in the first place is not wise. Sometimes circumstances may force a change. However, if it is only change for the sake of change, or it is change because the value of the original mission is not adequately understood, it is not necessary. If the direction of a company is changed and it is a targeted focus with absolute clarity – that organization will likely continue with success in its new direction.

However, if a change to the direction is made without that very necessary focus and clarity, or if there is no new vision and the old vision is left to evolve in any way - that anyone - finds appropriate, the organization will fail.

Where this is no vision, the people perish; … (Proverbs 29:18 – MKJV)

If your purpose is clear, examine the activities that your organization is currently engaged in. Are they focused on that purpose? On the other hand, do those initiatives have the potential to knock your company off course? Perhaps you will find that your organization has already steered off course. It is not too late to bring it back. If you are walking in the woods with a compass that is a few degrees off, you are still walking in the right direction in general and once the error is detected it should not take long to get back on course. Keep in mind that the longer that you have been off course – the further away from your destination you will be, and it will become increasingly more difficult to get back on course.

When an organization achieves absolute clarity of mission – throughout the ranks – and continues to focus on that purpose, that organization will achieve success. It is all but guaranteed. It is entirely the responsibility of the leader at the top to ensure this. If the leader does not – no one else is going to step in and do it for him or her. Evaluate your organization today against the principles of focus and clarity and if required, make any necessary changes to get it back on track.

The moment we begin to fear the opinions of others and hesitate to tell the truth that is in us, and from motives of policy are silent when we should speak, the divine floods of light and life no longer flow into our souls.

Elizabeth Cady Stanton (1815 - 1902), 1890

Chapter Three

LISTENING AND LEADING

"THE COMPANY"

When the results began to decline, and because there was no real true focus as described in the previous chapter, the continuous parade of changing leadership tried various strategies to kick-start the momentum. The strategies employed were almost always "in addition to" or "do more" types of add-on strategies. Many were focused on changing merchandise assortments and merchandise flow within stores. A certain amount of new technology was also employed. Some changes were made to the manner in which the company operates, but were usually governed by an individual's idea or opinion and not by what was best for the company as a whole.

The problem was that almost every strategy employed was under the assumption that the foundation of the company was sound – that everything worked fine – and it was only a new direction that was required. In other words, an assumption that the ship is in perfect running order – all the leader had to do was grab the wheel and steer it.

Each new leader would arrive on their shining white horse as the saviour of the company and before trying to understand the challenges, would begin making up and implementing strategies and changes. This approach would in due course result in frustration when the desired results were not achieved. That frustration would transfer to the entire organization in the form of blame for lack of execution and the constant need to push harder.

In reality the basics of the operation of the company were not in place – in fact they were in turmoil. Everything operated in isolation from each other. For example:

- Workload levels and payroll budgets were never compared – resulting in a constant flow of workload that exceeded the capacity to complete.

- Advertising and the buying to supply the goods for that advertising were not coordinated with each other – resulting in out of stocks on advertised goods and very dissatisfied customers.

- Desired "in-stock" rates and total inventory dollar management levels did not match – making it impossible to keep the stores "in-stock".

The new leader would yell, "go", but the organization could not get the engine started.

So why didn't the new leaders see it? Why couldn't they see the problems that existed and then first work to correct them? The reason is that the organization purposely hid it from them and failed to communicate the problems. Moreover, the reason for this monumental breakdown in communication is the consequence of leaders that did not really want to hear about the problems.

One of the leading causes of this organizations lack of success, and I suspect the same for many organizations, is the failure of the leadership to open their eyes and face the truth – to confront the brutal facts of their reality. There is certainly a time when you just have to say, "Get it done" and insist that the organization works through and solves the problems and issues that they face. There is a line defining the difference between real systemic problems and basic poor execution, which should not be crossed. However, this is not the state of affairs in this company. The numerous problems, because of being completely ignored for years have grown and extended deep far reaching roots into every area of the organization.

There were leaders that cultured an atmosphere of respect that still exists in the organization today. This was a welcome change from some of the tyrannical dictators who assumed the helm early in the 15-year doom loop. However, this culture of respect was without honesty. Speaking your mind – how you really feel – is political suicide in this company. This company is literally crippled by politics. I like the following definition of politics from the book "The Five Dysfunctions of a Team":[1]

Politics is when people choose their words and actions based on how they want others to react rather than based on what they really think.

Rarely in this company is someone asked for his or her opinion, and if they are – they will not give it – at least not honestly, due to fear. Any opinion given in "The Company" is a risk for two reasons:

- First – the manner in which the opinion is communicated is analysed and if the tone or words chosen are not polite (politically correct) enough – the opinion is for the most part, dismissed.
- Second, if the opinion is different – contrary or in objection to the norm – it is either deliberately perceived and understood incorrectly in order to fit it back into the box or, rationalized away and dismissed.

In both cases, the individual is labelled and after a certain amount of non-conforming or perceived impolite opinions – it is determined that they are not a fit in the organization and are exited.

There is no room for critical thinking and open honest communication in this organization. You will not find vigorous debate anywhere in this organization. The organization is filled with trained "yes" men and women who have pushed aside their ability to express any of their own differences of opinions.

No person is promoted to a senior position in the company unless they conform to the culture that is described above. If someone changes – they are quickly muffled or exited. The leadership team itself is paralysed by this culture and unable to express concerns among each other.

Over time, the system (or the machine as some like to call it), essentially the entire organization was adjusted to support this culture. Some examples:

- A suggestion program, which allowed any person in the organization to submit suggestions on how to improve the company, was eliminated. This very beneficial and successful program was in place for a long period of time before this – ten years that I am aware of – but perhaps even decades.

- Hierarchy (a level of bureaucracy) was put in place to filter communication between the stores and the merchandise buying office and replenishment divisions. Store Managers were no longer able (allowed) to speak directly to a buyer or replenishment manager about issues, ideas or suggestions they may have in their store. The implied intent was that communication would be more efficiently channelled through a team of people vs. every store manager calling, creating duplication. In the end, it was obvious that this "filter" was simply to get the customer (the stores in this case), along with their problems, off their [buying/replenishment silos] backs.

I suspect as you read this you can see how obvious the problems are and how easy they would be to detect and correct, which accurately reveals the blindness that occurs within the bureaucracy of organizations. These are only two examples – there are many more. Once again, many that work in the organization can see them – but if no one is willing to change them – it is easier to pretend that the problems do not exist in an attempt to maintain some sanity and job satisfaction. I think most find comfort by existing in a level of consciousness just below reality in order to continue to work and thrive in an organization that operates as this one does.

I will share one final story to illustrate the glaring lack of leadership and communication in "The Company". Since we are talking about a retail company with a large number of front line employees across many stores, it should not be hard to imagine that an employee discount benefit would be an important part of the compensation package. It was. However, one of the leaders during the 15-year doom loop – in an effort to stave off the continuing decline in profits – decided that the discount benefit was an area to look at to reduce expenses. Therefore, the leader at the time, not only reduced the overall benefit, but also changed and reduced the amount of discount on certain categories depending on their profitability. From a business perspective, you might be thinking that this was a good idea, as it would reduce costs. Your assumption would be incorrect. It is important to understand that the cost of this benefit – the cost to provide a discount to your best and most loyal advocates – is only a very small fraction of this company's overall mark down cost. Remember, that this very small fraction was only reduced – not eliminated. Therefore, in the end the <u>expected</u> savings was less than .1% of the overall markdown rate – an extremely insignificant amount. You may have noticed that the word expected was underlined – which I will explain.

This one act, to try to increase profits, in the end alienated the company's best customers – its own employees. A large majority of the employees of this company began to shop at "The Company's" main competitor – some because they could now get certain commodities cheaper, but most out of protest. This decision was made in unison with an equally shortsighted play on a customer rewards program that actually put the employees at a disadvantage compared to any other customer that was not an employee.

The entire organization was angry and completely disenchanted with the company for which they worked. Their loyalty was diluted. Sales decreased even further and the employee discount expressed as a rate to sales remained the same. There is no doubt that the overall discount benefit dollars spent was reduced. However, at a cost to the organization in top line sales and goodwill that is immeasurable. When your own employees are shopping at your competitor out of protest, you have to believe that something went terribly wrong.

Some years later, the company reversed some of these decisions but it was too little too late. Shopping patterns had been established outside of the organization. Bitterness continued, and continues to this day to lie just beneath the surface in the hearts and minds of many employees in this company because of this unbelievably ignorant decision. Everyone, and I mean everyone, below the top leaders in the organization knew that these changes were not a good idea. So how could it happen? If the leadership of the company were more in touch with the organization and the people in the organization – these kinds of decisions would have never been made.

The hit 1960's spy parody television show "Get Smart" starring Don Adams as Maxwell Smart (recently made into a movie - 2008), had a recurring sequence showing all of the important delegates, agents and the chief in a boardroom meeting. In order to maintain secrecy and keep the meeting confidential, a "cone of silence" was lowered over the heads of each of the individuals at the boardroom table. The humour in this sequence was that the "cone of silence" was so effective; each person could only hear him or her self and was impossible to hear anyone else that was sitting at the same table. They would all eventually get frustrated and the "cones of silence" were raised. As funny as this sequence in "Get

Smart" was, this is a great figurative analogy of "The Company's" communication practices.

❋❋❋❋❋❋❋❋

LEADERSHIP

Nearly all men can stand adversity, but if you want to test a man's character, give him power.
Abraham Lincoln (1809 - 1865)

Humility is the cornerstone of leadership. Humility is best defined as being without arrogance, showing modesty and not elevating ones self above anyone else in status. Humility is not depreciating or devaluing oneself in an attempt to bring others up. It is appreciating others as much as you appreciate yourself.

There is a great deal of evidence to support the idea that the most effective leaders are those that demonstrate humility. In his best selling book "Good to Great", Jim Collins describes the leaders of the most successful companies as "Level 5" leaders. He explains that "Level 5" leaders display both personal humility and professional will. They attribute success to others when things are going well, but when things are going poorly they look in the mirror at themselves.[2]

Jesus Christ, the most influential leader of all time consistently displayed the qualities of humility and servant hood. He introduced the radical concept of servant leadership by both teaching and leading by example, that those who desire to be the greatest – must become the servant of all.

I prefer the definition of leadership described by James C. Hunter in his book "The World's Most Powerful Leadership Principle – How to become a Servant Leader". His definition:
[3]

The skills of influencing people to enthusiastically work toward goals identified as being for the common good, with character that inspires confidence.

We have all been shaped by various styles of leadership throughout our lives. Our parents, siblings, friends, teachers, coaches, pastors, supervisors, bosses, elected government officials, etc. have all impacted us in varying degrees. We learn which styles of leadership we appreciate and of course, those methods that we do not prefer. I would suspect that if you were to think about the most influential leaders in your own life – those that you appreciate the most and aspire to become like – you would find the approaches to leadership utilized by them, in many ways matches the description of leadership that I have previously provided.

When they discover the center of the universe, a lot of people will be disappointed to discover they are not it.
Bernard Bailey

With the exception of perhaps a few fortunate people, we have all been exposed to the leader on the opposite end of the spectrum. We must still call them leaders because they do influence people – just not in a way that is empowering. These types of leaders seem to think that they have all the answers. Some think they even have all the questions. They think they know what is best for everyone, you and the organization. Many are arrogant and hold themselves elevated far above the "commoner" in the organization. Their contempt and condescending tone brings their obvious lack of respect to light. Many display a dictatorial style of leadership and run their organization with an iron fist. These leaders literally suck the life out of everyone in the organization.

You do not lead by hitting people over the head - that's assault, not leadership.
Dwight D. Eisenhower

The key to successful leadership today is influence, not authority.
Kenneth Blanchard

There are arguably more books written on the topic of leadership than any other subject, all of them revealing the acquired knowledge and experience of the authors. My experience overwhelmingly reveals that only those leaders that exhibit humility in their leadership style achieve lasting success. Conversely, the leaders that exhibit arrogance and the know-it-all attitude never achieve lasting success. They may fly under the radar for a time and might even achieve temporary success, but it is never sustained.

What you always do before you make a decision is consult. The best public policy is made when you are listening to people who are going to be impacted. Then, once policy is determined, you call on them to help you sell it.
Elizabeth Dole

Good leaders listen. They understand that they do not have all the answers. They acknowledge their distance from the customer and respect the opinions of those that are closest to the customer.

Unfortunately, when things are not working I.e.: results

are poor and not improving, strategies are not being implemented, goals are not being achieved - leaders often do the opposite of what they should be doing. They:

- Set the direction without any input from those that are closest to the customer
- Close down the lines of communication
- Become more forceful – as if it (the difficulties) were only a "lack of execution" issue

These approaches suggest that the problem lies everywhere else – that it is not you the leader, but rather the organization and everyone in it – and it is now time for you to take over and fix it.

Good leaders do the opposite. They look within themselves first, but not for all the answers. Instead they question what it is they have done, or are not doing that has caused the current problems. They hold themselves personally responsible – rather than everyone else. They are not too proud to seek the opinions from others – to ask for help. Society has a way of teaching us that asking for help is a sign of weakness. The trait of humility found in good leaders allows them to seek help. In reality, asking for help is a sign of strength.

LISTENING

Listen. Do not have an opinion while you listen because frankly, your opinion doesn't hold much water outside of Your Universe. Just listen. Listen until their brain has been twisted like a dripping towel and what they have to say is all over the floor.
Hugh Elliott, Standing Room Only weblog, 02-14-2003

We live in a world where everyone is desperate to be heard. The reason is that so few are actually listening. Listening is not just hearing. In fact, it does not even start with hearing. True listening starts with desire – a real desire to understand thoroughly what is being communicated. And when I develop and exercise that desire, I begin to use my intuition in combination with that desire, and only then, can I truly listen. Intuition is the state of being aware of or knowing something without having to discover or perceive it

If we are honest with ourselves, most of us are not really listening at all. While a point of view is being communicated to us, we are quickly accessing our point of view on the same subject and formulating our response before even hearing or considering the other side. We are listening only to respond.

With a desire to understand another person's point of view, we listen actively; which means that we probe in areas where further clarification is needed as well as repeat or paraphrase back what is being heard to clarify and acknowledge understanding. We listen for the "between the lines clues" – those signs of body language (increased passion in their voice, hand gestures, etc.) and seek to find out what is hidden. We consider their background, previous conversations, their "track record", etc. to understand their point of view more effectively. Sometimes, verbal communication is not even necessary to hear effectively. Actions often speak volumes and our intuition can perceive accurately what is being said – if we are listening. We have all heard the saying "actions speak louder than words."

Seek first to understand, then to be understood.
Stephen Covey

True listening is one of the most exhausting mental exercises one can do. The ability to take ones own agenda out of their mind and unselfishly focus on another without letting his or her mind wander to the cares of the day, is incredibly draining. It is also extraordinarily rewarding and productive. More problems can be solved with true listening than anything else.

Since we all desire to be heard, someone will have to take a step down, by putting their agenda or opinion onto the back burner, and seek to hear another's point of view. That takes humility. Those that do this are the most effective as leaders.

A good listener is a good talker with a sore throat.
Katharine Whitehorn

FRONT LINE EMPLOYEES HAVE THE ANSWERS

You never really hear the truth from your subordinates until after 10 in the evening.
Jurgen Schrempp, Former CEO of DaimlerChrysler

Strong leaders understand their strengths and weaknesses. They do what they do best and to compensate where they are not strong – they surround themselves with others that are talented in those areas of personal weakness. In other words, they face the fact and the reality that no one is good at everything.

They also recognize that a distance exists between them and the customer and that this distance grows larger as the organization grows. This distance makes it difficult to understand what the concerns and needs of the customer are. Because of this understanding, they keep in touch with those that are on the front lines of the business – those that interact with the customer. Most importantly, they listen – really listen, in order to understand and make changes that are in the best interest of the customer.

In the last two years, "The Company" once again opened up a line of communication that allowed anyone in the organization to communicate ideas and suggestions to the top levels of the organization. This was a great step and there has been acceptance and reaction to some of those suggestions. Take for example the discount story mentioned previously; it was via this new communication channel that the most recent leadership heard from literally hundreds of employees about their continued anger over that change (which was 4 years previous), and then reacted by making some reversals of the original decision. But the "leadership knows best" agenda still overshadowed most suggestions and because they were not seen as advantageous due to the glaring lack of focus and clarity (how do you know what is a good or bad suggestion if you don't even know what you are supposed to be doing in the first place), most were not implemented. Rationalization in this company is easier than making large-scale changes even if they are in the best interest of the customer. A word of advice: developing happy and engaged employees is always in the best interest of the customer and an excellent way to do that is to listen and implement every one of their worthy suggestions.

Good leaders listen to understand and because they operate from a place of humility, they know that they do not have all the answers. They know that they do not even have all the questions. When you ask for input, you will often receive more questions than answers. Why don't we ...? What is the reason for ...? When will ...? Etc. Sometimes the answers are in the questions themselves. I.e.: Why don't we provide a delivery service? Sometimes the leader will be able to provide the answer. However, in most cases the front line associate asks the question first only to illustrate the problem. They already have the answer or solution to the problem. And because they know the questions better than anyone since they hear directly from many customers – they have the best solutions.

If your customers are telling you something that either aggravates them or are suggesting an idea that would allow you to serve them better, why would you not want to grant their request. The best way to listen to your customers is to listen to your front line staff. Customer surveys and opinion polls will certainly give you good information in this regard, but we need to remember that most customers will not complete these. In addition, the customer will often only provide you with the problem. The front line associate, on the other hand, has the benefit of hearing directly from the customer and in particular, hearing the customer's emotion when they express their concerns to them. As well, they understand the inner workings of the company, and when combined with the previously mentioned customer feedback, it enables them to provide the most creative of solutions.

Unfortunately, as mentioned earlier, some leaders see this [asking others for the answers] as a sign of weakness. You are still their leader and they still want you to lead. They just want to offer their input when things are not as good as they could be or help to make the good even better.

BE WARY OF "YES" PEOPLE

If everyone is thinking alike – then somebody isn't thinking.
G. S. Patton

When two men in business always agree, one of them is unnecessary.
William Wrigley Jr. (1861 - 1932)

In any organization, the art of politics is a very dangerous thing. This lack of honesty can and does stop progress and bring organizations to a standstill. It is possible to communicate in a respectful way and still be honest. Despite this respect, sometimes people will get offended – there may be conflict and this is ok. In fact, if there is no conflict – there is a problem.

Relationships do not grow without conflict. Conflict, handled properly, allows relationships to move to a deeper level. A marriage without conflict will not be a marriage for long. I am not speaking of physical conflict or abuse – this is never necessary, healthy or productive. The conflict that I am suggesting is differences of opinion, disagreements and even misunderstandings – because misunderstandings that are never discussed will likely always remain a misunderstanding. It includes vigorous debate and discussion and may often even look like an argument. Healthy conflict gets issues and disputes out on the table, allows every opinion to be heard and considered and ends in unity and harmony with resolution of the issues. Organizations that do not experience healthy conflict will never achieve real lasting success.

Conflict is the gadfly of thought. It stirs us to observation and memory. It instigates to invention. It shocks us out of sheeplike passivity, and sets us at noting and contriving.
John Dewey

It is impossible for any group of people to agree with each other all the time. The different backgrounds, work experience, education, etc. allow for a dynamic array of thinking and ideas. To smother and choke the creative thinking and ideas from people in an organization is simply self-destructive. Yet, many organizations like "The Company" have done this. "The Company" is filled with individuals that I call "yes people". "Yes people" always agree. They never think anything is a bad idea. They never challenge and never question. They are the opposite of critical thinkers. "Yes people" are not born this way. Rather they are created from the fear of stating ones opinion that is uncompromisingly cultivated in many organizations. They are trained to believe that stating their opinion makes them a negative person. Since "Yes" people are always out to please, and it would seem at any cost; some have no problem making decisions that raise questions about their integrity. We will look at the practices of subtle deceit in more detail in a later chapter. Without treatment this "disease to please" will continue to spread and could be potentially terminal to an organization.

I cannot give you the formula for success, but I can give you the formula for failure: which is: Try to please everybody.
Herbert B. Swope

A common practice among many organizations is the tradition of calling problems – "opportunities" in an attempt to spin them in a positive light. This tendency to spin every problem into a positive light actually prolongs the solution. There is typically less urgency required in taking advantage of opportunities vs. tackling problems. Call them as they are.

Strong organizations look for the truth. They look for the root of the problem rather than just the symptoms. They look for and provide opportunities for everyone to be heard in this quest for the truth. "Politicking" is not substantial in strong organizations, at least not at a suppressing level. If something is not working – they confront the brutal facts. They face reality and do not hide from the truth. Vigorous debate is the norm. Opinions are expressed – everyone gets their say. They open all of the complex issues or proverbial "cans of worms".

Conflict happens whenever necessary. From an outsider's perspective, this may even look like undisciplined chaos. However, when handled properly – these organizations get at the truth or the root of the problem and quickly move to solutions. Finally, those solutions are put in place with lightning speed simply because everyone had the opportunity to express their opinions and participate and consequently feels valued.

Never apologize for showing feeling. When you do so, you apologize for the truth.
Benjamin Disraeli

CULTURE

Culture is the shared beliefs, customs, practices and social behaviours of an organization. It takes a humble leader to create a culture as described in the paragraph above – one who is willing to accept a challenge to his or her opinion and who carries a desire to hear everyone's viewpoint. Egotistical leaders encourage the opposite – universal agreement is expected. This type of leader, that has a low self-esteem, coerces opinions from others. Challenging this type of leader's opinion is seen as challenging their authority and will be met with certain punishment.

Culture is mostly unwritten and unsaid – it is just the way it is – and is created over time through events and experiences. Leadership positions at all levels are selected based on the existing culture. If the candidate does not fit the culture – he/she is usually passed over. This ensures that the culture remains constant – a form of self-preservation. As a result, it is extremely hard to change culture. It will take someone to stick his or her hand in the spoke of the spinning wheel of culture to undertake any change to it. A new leader that endeavours to do this may very well get their hand cut off. The longer that culture has been allowed to grow; the more ingrained it will be in the organization and the harder it will be to change.

Despite the enormity of the task to change culture, it is my opinion that if your organization is anything like "The Company", you will never achieve any real lasting success until you do change it. No brilliant strategy or perfect economy will allow an organization that is not honest with itself to survive.

To be clear, culture will never change without the expressed initiative and effort of the leader at the very top of any organization. Culture is both established and reinforced from the top of the organization. The entire organization styles their own beliefs, customs and practices from their observations of the top leader in the organization. It truly rolls downhill.

◻◻◻◻◻

Good leaders cultivate honest speech; they love advisors who tell them the truth. (Proverbs 16:13 - MSG)

It will take a genuine humility in the leaders of an organization to allow for a willingness to hear and accept the opinions of others. When the leader values the opinions of others in an organization regardless of their title or level of tenure, it creates an atmosphere of cooperation and teamwork. On the other hand, when we are hung up on the "niceties" of communication and company etiquette at the expense of critical thinking, creativity is quickly shut down. The "yes" people will always rise up in these situations to support and substantiate that culture. Leaders that desire "subjects" rather than team members will not only welcome this support but will encourage it. Only staunch determination will be able to change a culture that has been tainted by this disease, and a successful change in this regard will require a pulling of roots that will shake the very foundation of that organization. It will not be easy, but most things that are worthwhile rarely are.

I have always maintained that all any new president (leader) of "The Company" had to do was take the time to meet with the people at all levels of the organization to get their input on what needed to be done in order to make the organization successful. Then by taking those ideas and implementing them, "The Company" would see immediate success and that leader would be viewed as a brilliant individual. However, it would take humility to do this – and the culture of "The Company" does not allow for that characteristic in their leadership. Please do not make the same mistake in your organization. If you already have this type of culture – do whatever you have to in order to change it. In addition, there is no downside to listening to your people, using their opinions and ideas to help shape your strategy and implement their worthy suggestions.

Nothing astonishes men so much as common sense and plain dealing.

Ralph Waldo Emerson (1803 - 1882), 'Art,' 1841

Chapter Four

CUSTOMER FOCUSED

"THE COMPANY"

During a store tour with the company president, we spoke to an employee that worked in the food services department of one of the stores. The president asked if there was anything that he could do to help the employee carryout their job more effectively. The associate responded with a request that we offer diabetic jams to serve the numerous senior customers that frequented the restaurant. The president responded with "We don't want to do that because they (seniors) are not really our target customer."

I was there. I heard these words come out of his mouth. The reality is that "seniors" are a part of this company's customer base. In fact, as we move forward into the future – the senior customer will become a bigger part of this and many other companies's customer base – with or without diabetes.

The issue here is not about diabetic jam – but rather of a leader that could not see the forest for the trees. Fortunately, for "The Company", and the senior customer, this president has moved on – and is now most likely benefiting from those special discounts one begins to receive at the age of 55. I wonder if his perspective has changed.

Approximately half way through the 15-year doom loop, "The Company" decided to get serious about providing better customer service. A major customer service initiative was thrust that included both organizational structure changes at store level, and extensive training programs. The initiative included check and follow-up systems to ensure continued progress. The program was substantial enough to make changes to the culture that existed.

The front line associates absolutely loved it. They knew we were on the right track and expressed that fact openly and frequently. During a meeting with the associates in one store I was personally told, "This is exactly what our customers are looking for – this is great. Please don't screw this up and let this become just another flavour of the month." Customer response was equally as impressive. The customer noticed and began to look at the company as their destination to shop again.

This positive momentum lasted approximately two years and then "The Company" did "screw it up". The destruction of the initiative began when decisions were made outside of the new customer service mindset – decisions that prevented the front line associates from providing the great service that everyone desired to give. The reason for the end of a very positive and effective customer service thrust is explained in the next three paragraphs but can really be summed up in the failure of leadership.

That renewed thrust for improved "service providing" was the brainchild of one executive. Unfortunately, his position was one level too low. He was the VP of store operations – reporting to the president. While he had permission to initiate a new service mindset – he did not have complete buy in. Permission is like saying, "Ok, I will let you try your experiment". The reality is that as soon as some adversity hit – which always eventually does – that consent was easily withdrawn. In absence of a detailed explanation, I think that I only need to inform you that this was the same president in charge of the company at that time that I referred to in the opening story of this chapter. Because there was not complete support at the top of the organization, the initiative (customer service initiative) only lived and breathed in one silo – the store operations silo – or within itself in the stores. If you had to pick one place to implement a customer service strategy – this would be it. However, if the other parts or divisions of the company are not on side (particularly the top leadership) – there is a ceiling to the level of service that an organization as a whole can achieve.

During the time of this "customer service initiative", there would be quarterly updates on the progress. Everyone (in the other silos) would consistently applaud the great service improvements that were realized and reported on at store level. Surprisingly, it never occurred to the majority that good customer service should exist at all levels in the organization – at least not in any tangible way. This company believes that customer service is the sole responsibility of the front line associate – the person that is face to face with the customer. They (the leadership of "The Company") do not believe that anyone outside of the front line associate should have any responsibility to the customer. When I say believe, I am cutting through all rhetoric and stating the actual outcome – the truth and not what is just preached without the leadership and desire to see practiced.

Part of this customer service thrust was to find a way to measure the level of service that was being provided. A third party customer survey company was utilized in this regard. Useful information was collected directly from the customer continuously via a survey mechanism initiated at the point of sale (checkout), in order to improve the level of service. Customers do not care what part of the organization is responsible for a problem they encounter – they tell it like it is. Much of the information collected was store focused and useful for store teams to work on. In addition there was also a great deal of information collected and reported that was focused on buying, marketing, replenishment and other divisions of the organization. It was assumed in the store operations group that everyone (all divisions) were working to improve their level of service based on the customer feedback that they received. That assumption would prove to be incorrect. In reality, during the 2-3 years that we collected this information, none of it was communicated to any level or division of the organization other than the stores themselves. All suggestions for improvements to any area other than the stores were lost in electronic heaven.

This customer survey mechanism was for the most part an exercise to exhibit the desired customer service optics that seems to be so important to every organization in the service sector. Thus the unspoken belief "If your company is not seen by the public as customer focused – then it must not be".

"The Company" – a retail organization – existed to meet the basic wants and needs of the customer's everyday life. To meet those basic wants and needs satisfactorily, the merchandise must be available to the customer when she/he comes in to purchase. This is about as basic as it gets. However, "The Company" failed miserably on this fundamental component of their business. Since this is their business – how they intend to make their profit, it is not only surprising but also shocking that they (retail company) would not target this as priority number one. As you read the analysis and observations of this company in this book, it will become apparent that "leadership" is the root of every one of the problems that will be identified. The problem of "in-stock" (available merchandise for purchase) is certainly no exception.

The barrier in this case is best summarized as the inability to confront the brutal facts as discussed in the previous chapter. The issue was not completely ignored – there was an understanding that the level of "in-stock" was less than ideal. Various solutions were thrown at the problem, but each was a "band aid" of sorts – treating symptoms and not getting anywhere near the root of the problem. The machine (bureaucracy of the organization) fortified the silo walls between themselves to deflect blame for the problem. The "supply chain" division – which is responsible for this problem – created reports to show over-inflated "in-stock" rates (a measurement of item availability for sale to the customer) in order to satisfy the concern. This was done by showing an "on-hand" (quantity of any item that was "on-hand" in the store) of <u>one unit</u> to be completely "in-stock". In reality if that particular item had a rate of sale of any amount greater than one for every two weeks of time – it would be impossible to replenish in time to prevent from selling out. In other words, the report was duplicitous and was used to deceive. Subsequently, fictitious "on-hand" quantities, without the corresponding inventory, were pushed through the computer system to enhance the reporting on "in-stock" without having to spend inventory dollars that were not available – another deception to protect a silo. "Yes" people become very creative when faced with competing pressures. The sad fact is that all of *these* games that "The Company" played continued to slash into their ability to provide product to the customer.

Decisions made in "The Company" were not often made in the best interest of the customer. They were almost always made based on financial results. Not that there is anything wrong with that – the financial health of the organization should definitely be a consideration. However, the financial numbers should not consistently trump the wishes of the customer. In fact granting the wishes of the customer often leads to the best financial results possible.

Probably the most vivid example of this is with the price file system. This is the system that you the customer would interact with whenever you purchase something. The system brings up the price you pay on each item you purchase. The technology (technical equipment – computers, cash register systems, software, etc.) in "The Company" has become somewhat outdated. (It is financially difficult to keep your technology up to date if you are not making any money). The point of sale register system holds a finite amount of information. When the system was created – more than a decade earlier, the storage space was sufficient – but not any longer. Any item that was advertised and put on sale at a lower price had to be entered into the system in order for that price to automatically be provided to the customer when it was purchased. "The Company" continued to advertise items and commodities beyond what it could fit in the price file system. It was decided and expected that the cashiers would detect and catch what was on sale and provide that sale price to the customer manually. However, because of the thousands of items advertised on any given week, the cashiers did not always catch the sale price and the customers were often overcharged. Many of us can remember a time when they were overcharged by a store and how violated it made us feel. Unfortunately, in Canada, "The Company" has been public offender #1 in this area.

The fix would have been to ticket the merchandise manually to a new lower price. However, by doing this, the markdowns are entered all at once showing a large financial hit to the books vs. taking the markdown only when an item is sold resulting in much more gradual financial impact. Hence, a decision made continuously based on financials despite a loud and clear message that this was a major source of aggravation from the customer.

In June 2002, the Competition Bureau of Canada endorsed the Scanner Price Accuracy Voluntary Code, which evolved from the collaborative efforts of the Retail Council of Canada, the Canadian Association of Chain Drug Stores, the Canadian Federation of Independent Grocers and the Canadian Council of Grocery Distributors. These associations are composed of national, regional and local retailers selling a wide assortment of general merchandise, as well as pharmaceutical and food products. The code is a commitment on the part of the retailer to the accuracy of scanning on the goods that they sell. It is a promise that says "what the items are signed or ticketed at will be the same that they are scanned at when you pay for them, and if it does not scan accurately and the item scanned comes up at a higher price, we will provide you with that item for free (up to a $10.00 maximum)."[1] Patrons of Canadian retailers may recall the various forms of signs that are displayed in stores explaining this code and promise.

A report published in September 2007, by the group of retail associations mentioned above states that among the three retail sectors and four associations, 2,698 companies representing over 8,000 retail locations support the Code. The report also indicates the continued year over year improvements in pricing accuracy realized by these participating companies.[2]

Unfortunately, "The Company" decided not to participate in this "voluntary" program. Supporting this code would have caused "The Company" to incur significant costs through the giving away of free product due to scanning errors. However, it would have also forced it to focus on and correct the monumental scanning and pricing errors that exist.

When an organization lacks vision and has only a short-sighted narrow view they will often make decisions to deliver positive short-term results at the expense of sustained long-term success. It is the difference between just doing things right or doing the right thing.

❋❋❋❋❋❋❋❋

What is customer service?

At its basic core, customer service is simply solving problems. The problems in this case are not always simple problems that require solutions, but are more often and better described as the "wants & needs" of life.

Therefore, people (customers) have problems (wants & needs) for which they need solutions, and businesses are created to solve those problems. For example:

- The problem of providing food for one's family is solved by various grocery retailers.
- The problem of transportation is solved by car manufacturers, or companies that provide public transportation – bus, plane, train etc.
- Health care providers best solve the problem of an illness.

Often, businesses introduce people to problems that they did not even know that they had. Take the industry of cell phones as an example. We did not really even realize the monumental void in communication that we were forced to live with since the dawn of time until the cellular phone was introduced. I am not sure how we ever survived without the ability to talk to almost anyone from anywhere at anytime. Fortunately, that problem – now astoundingly evident – has been solved by the various cellular phone providers.

Since all businesses and organizations start with the idea or concept of solving such problems in the first place, they would be wise to never forget this as they grow. These are the basics of the business – the absolute core - and without them, there is no business or reason to exist. Organizations that forget their purpose – their reason for existence – ultimately forget their customers and that which they originally set out to do for them.

WHO IS THE CUSTOMER?

From the perspective of marketing, your customer is defined in any way that you want. You could target a specific gender, age group, market niche, ethnic group etc. These are the individuals that you endeavour to serve. However, in reality for those businesses and organizations that are already running, the customer is whomever you are serving. That is, whoever is patronizing your establishment – buying your product – using your services – or seeking your assistance. Despite an organization's efforts in marketing to attract their target customer, it cannot afford to push away any person or group that is willing to buy their product or use their services, unless of course, business is so good that customers need to be refused. This certainly is not the case for "The Company" in reference to the story at the opening of this chapter.

I suspect that some would disagree with what they have read in the previous paragraph based on the "Pareto principle". The "Pareto principle" (also known as the 80-20 rule, the law of the vital few and the principle of factor sparsity) states that; for many events, 80% of the effects come from 20% of the causes.[3] If we apply the "Pareto principle" to marketing, we would say that "20% of your customers will provide 80% of your profits" and therefore businesses should focus their marketing and customer service on that 20%. I am not suggesting otherwise. However;

1. If your business is struggling – I.e.: scraping rock bottom trying to stay afloat – you are probably not in a position to exclude certain customers. You may not even be clear on who your best customers are.

2. If your business is thriving, it does not mean that you should push the 80% away. You do not deny any service simply because they are not your most profitable customers – or they are not your target customer (as in the case with seniors and diabetic jam).

The customer is most often referred to as the person that is providing revenue or taking advantage of your organization's services. However, those within the organization are also customers to each other. In a retail organization:

- The buyers serve the stores by providing them with goods to sell and the stores serve the buyers by advising them of the trends in their markets.
- Transportation/logistics serve stores through the delivery of goods in a timely and efficient manner.
- Marketing serves the organization by drawing an increasing number of customers to the organization.

You can adapt similar links in any organization but in the end, each person ultimately serves the front line customer for which the organization exists, some directly – others indirectly. It is crucial for every person in an organization to understand, embrace and act on this principle. It may sound painfully obvious, but I come from a company that has completely lost sight of this. Moreover, I am not talking about spewing polite and friendly but meaningless lip service. Rather a deep-seated willingness to do what is best for the customer through whatever channel or means available.

CUSTOMER SERVICE IS NOT A PROGRAM

Many organizations create a program or a system, put it in a binder or training video, send it out to the masses, then dust off their hands, and proclaim that customer service is now in place. They soon discover that not much has changed. It is not possible to simply tell, will or insist that good customer service be provided. Providing service is an attitude and a deep-seated belief within the individual. It can be inspired but first comes from inside of a person. In other words, customer service is not something that can simply be taught. While training (teaching) may have a positive effect on the service that your customers receive, it will never become great service. Great service must uniquely come out of each individual.

Service is defined in the dictionary as "the occupation of a servant". Servant is defined as "one who serves others". To serve is to help – to wait on – to supply or furnish with something. Not everyone understands how to provide service for another. Individuals that are selfish in nature do not intuitively understand how to serve others. It is not just that they have not experienced it (serving others), they don't get it [serving] - it doesn't do anything for them – doesn't stimulate them in any way or make them feel good. It is not my intent to judge, but if an organization is expecting them [selfish people] to become "service minded" while they are at work, there is going to be disappointment.

An important component of recruitment and hiring for

any organization should focus on trying to find people that are giving and unselfish. This is necessary for any front line position that deals directly with the outside customer. Based on my argument above – that every person in any organization ultimately serves the customer – it (striving to find selfless and considerate people) should be a focus in the hiring for any position.

It is not that difficult to detect an unselfish nature in people. The area of the resume – "Interests & activities" – which little time and attention is given, will tell you a great deal about a person's nature. If the list includes any type of volunteering it would be a good indication of an unselfish person. Simple questions during an interview can quickly establish a person's nature in this regard. With a clear desire to identify unselfishness, any conversation with an interview type tone will reveal it. If it is not exposed – does not come out, chances are that it does not exist. If you start with an organization full of giving, generous individuals, customer service will for the most part, come naturally if the organization does not inadvertently smother it.

Once you have people with the right attitude, companies should set the expectation, empower them and then get out of their way. Clarifications on issues such as the following are critical:

- What are your organizations expectations for service?

- Do you want your people to solve every problem and satisfy every customer on their own, or do you expect them to ask you first?

- Is there a dollar amount that they can spend in the objective of satisfying a customer?

You need to clearly outline what you will allow them to do on their own and draw the line as to when and where they should seek approval. Where you draw that line is extremely important. The level of empowerment and authority that you extend outward will be the difference between a company that provides great customer service and one that is full of demoralized employees – the difference between an organization that thrives and one that is working just to survive.

The level of authority and ability that the individuals in your organization have to solve problems and satisfy customers <u>on their own</u>, equals the level of engagement (satisfaction) that they will have in their job and the quality of service provided to your customers.

If you treat your employees like the competent, capable people that they are – they will respond positively in a number of ways in return to you, your company and the customers that patronize your company. Not allowing any latitude and empowerment in decision-making and resolving customer issues demonstrates a lack of trust in the competence of the people in your organization. If you do not believe that they are competent – why did you hire them in the first place? I have found that people generally rise to the level of expectation that is put on them. They want more responsibility – it makes them feel important – it makes them feel that they are contributing more. I have found that the more (authority/empowerment) that you give them – the more they take and want to take. Their engagement increases and as a result, they are happier, work harder, contribute more and remain in your organization longer. It takes a strong leader to create this type of empowerment and autonomy for their organization. The perception might be that the leader relinquishes power as they extend more and more authority down through the ranks. The leader with a low self-esteem in this case would feel threatened and both consciously and unconsciously thwart it at all costs. The reality is that the leader that allows increased authority and responsibility gains more power and it also comes with more respect. Here again it comes back to leadership.

Trust men and they will be true to you; treat them greatly, and they will show themselves great.
Ralph Waldo Emerson (1803 - 1882), Essays, First Series: Prudence, 1841

When you extend the necessary empowerment and authority, you do not have to tell them *how*. Let them marvel you with their creativeness and ingenuity. In fact, you will need to work frequently at removing more and more of the barriers and boundaries that will keep them restrained. Eliminate all bureaucracy that would restrict anyone in the organization from the perspective of providing great customer service. There should not be a "box" that requires individuals to work outside of. In other words – simply "get out of their way"!

To touch on an example mentioned at the start of this chapter; the price file system – a company should never employ a system/procedure, or adopt a policy that has the potential to alienate even one customer. "The Company" was aware that this was upsetting their customers. Nevertheless, they once again failed to face the truth – confront the brutal facts because they would have had to change direction and make a different decision that could cause discomfort. They chose to do things right (in their minds) rather than to do the right thing. If you have something in place that is causing, or has the potential to cause a single customer to become alienated from your organization – change it as quickly as possible.

STORY TELLING

The only "program" a company should have to drive customer service is "story telling". There is no better way to illustrate how to give great customer service than to tell a real story of a situation where great customer service has been given. Share stories of great service, both from your organization as well as others, to continuously inspire.

Here are three personal stories that show very different elements of great customer service: 1) Exemplary after sales service, 2) exemplary pre-sale service 3, consistently good service.

I own a small Clarke (brand name) air compressor, which powers my brad nailer that I use for smaller building projects around the house. I somehow managed to break the pressure regulator off of the air compressor. I called the 1-800 number in my owners manual to obtain a replacement for the broken piece. I spoke to a man named Rob who quickly advised that the new part would be $30. Then he advised that if I wanted, he could send me a used one – no cost. I of course agreed and provided my address. The part arrived the next day – free – no charges for shipping. My compressor was no longer under warranty, nor should the part be covered under warranty even if it had been as I was the one who damaged it. I don't know exactly why they have used parts at Superior Fasteners – Clarke power products. I do know that they have superior after sales service and will definitely buy my next air tools with their name on it.

I am a "do-it-yourselfer". I wanted to put soffitt and trim on the bottom of my deck, but I had never completed that kind of work previously. I asked for a quote to have it done for me. The quote for $1,600 (my deck is not very big 9x10) inspired me to learn how to do it myself. I phoned around and was getting frustrated with the lack of information that I was finding until I spoke to Randy at local siding establishment (All-side Contracting – Edmonton Alberta, Canada). He told me to come down and he would help me out. He spent well over an hour with me telling me exactly what I needed and how to put it up. He did not get impatient with me (at least he didn't show it anyway), when I asked questions about the "siding and soffitt" terminology or "lingo" that was foreign to me. In the end, the job cost me $300 – materials only and with his instruction, it was not only easy – but I had fun doing it. Randy was willing to give up over an hour of his time to help me out on a sale that was likely one of the smallest he had ever written.

There are many options for hardware stores around my home. Since I do a great deal of "do-it-yourself" work, I do my share of shopping for material. Over time after comparing prices, service, assortment, and "in-stock" levels – I have gravitated to one store – Totem (Alberta, Canada – home building/hardware chain). They always have what I need. It is generally cheaper than the competition. They provide prompt knowledgeable service. I never have to wait in line, and they even have free popcorn in-store. I go there exclusively now because of their consistent solid performance.

Customer service is meeting the needs or solving the problems that your customer has. Identifying who your customer is in addition to their needs (problems) is the key to providing the right service.

Providing world-class customer service is not a program or system. Great service is rooted in people – people with a willingness to serve. Organizations usually do more to hinder and suppress the ability and initiative of their people to provide top quality service with rules and restrictions. They should instead focus on extending authority and empowerment and then get out of their way allowing them latitude to exercise that authority. The level of engagement among a company's employees is very closely aligned to the amount of responsibility and empowerment that is extended to them, and the higher the engagement level of employees, the lower the turnover.

I cannot imagine any company starts without a desire to provide the best customer service possible. As organizations grow and become more complicated, programs and processes start to take over and providing great customer service is often only assumed to be happening by the leadership. The well used terms of "Customer Focused" or "Customer Centric" is exactly that – having the customer in the centre of everything that you do. Unfortunately, in many companies these terms are not an indication of reality.

Organizations and companies need to get back to their grass roots, the reason that they exist and that solution for their customers for with which they began. Those organizations that continue to focus on true customer service as a mindset rather than a slogan or a program will thrive. They would never make a decision that has the potential to alienate even one of their customers.

A leader needs to "let go" in order to stimulate great customer service and allow it to prevail. Trust will need to be extended; a trust that allows liberal and unrestrictive guidelines for an organization to satisfy the customer that says; "I have confidence in your decision making ability and give you total authority to go above and beyond to satisfy the needs and wants of customers of this company." Those leaders that can go beyond just lip service in this area and back their words and commitments will most certainly lead their organization to sustained success.

We are drowning in information but starved for knowledge.

John Naisbit

Chapter Five

DON'T LET THE "ACCOUNTANTS" TAKE OVER

"THE COMPANY"

In the former time when "The Company" experienced immense success, the organization was run by the "store operations" division who were the "merchandisers" or "operators". As the name implies, this is the division of the company that is commonly known as the "stores" comprising of the store managers up to the vice president of store operations. Because this division was the closest to the customer, their decisions and strategies were closely aligned to what the customer wanted. To clarify the statement "was run" – I mean this division had the most power. The top leader (president) at the time understood where the revenue to the organization came from and made it a priority to give what the customer wanted by allowing or accepting the direction to come from the "store operations" division. Provide what the customer wants and you will be successful - this of course is not rocket science but rather common sense and a message now repeated throughout this book. It is also worth mentioning that this is the time in "The Company's" history that it produced some of its greatest success – once again - when driven and led by the "Stores".

The illustration below shows visually that the "store operations" group was the centre of the organization with the other divisions positioned to support.

DON'T LET THE "ACCOUNTANTS" TAKE OVER

When the leadership of that time changed, the new president favoured a much different view of how to operate the company. Since his background was in the "buying" division, he felt that it was all about the buy or the merchandise that "The Company" had to sell. It seemed that he felt as long as "The Company" had the right merchandise; nothing else could prevent the customers from breaking down the doors wanting to purchase it. This logic may have worked if it (the merchandise) was must have items such as high tech gadgetry, and there was no other competition. However, that was not the reality with "The Company" – there was an abundance of competition offering the same or similar goods.

The illustration on the next page shows how the company was structured very early in the 15 years of waning success – the doom loop. The "buying" division moved to the centre of the organization and the "store operations" became a support function.

It is important to note when viewing this diagram (next page) from the perspective of revenue generation – the only circle that revenue is generated within is "store operations". The problems started in this company when the bread and butter of the organization – the only area that brings in revenue - was pushed to the periphery. (I have purposely left the "credit division" off of this diagram for the reason that credit is not a revenue generating activity, but a profit centre.)

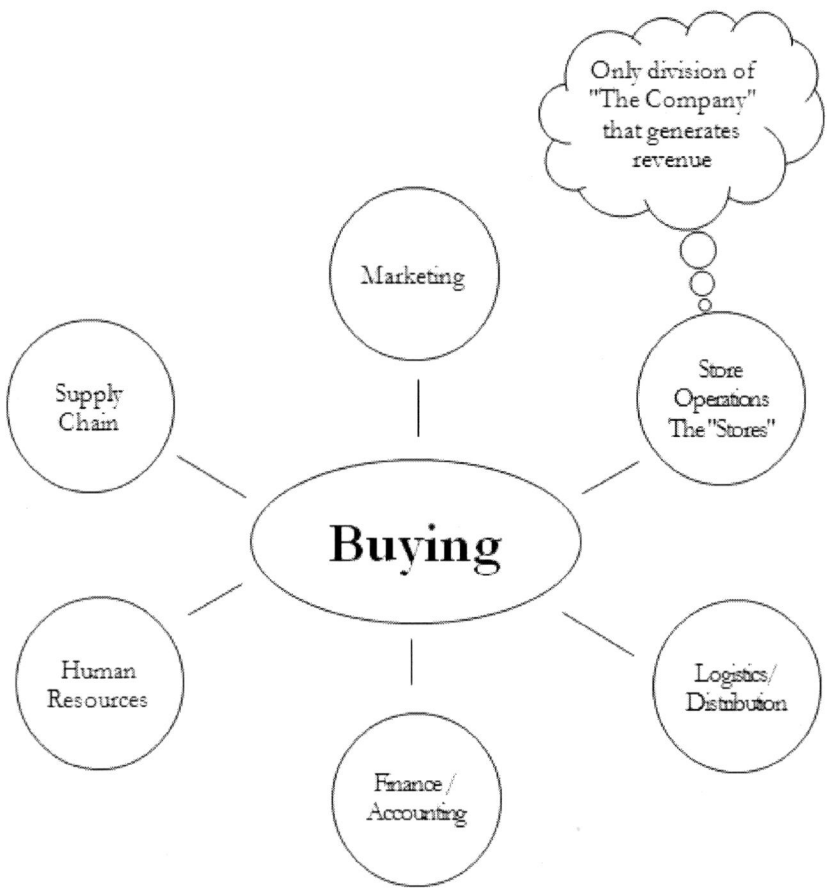

Another president later - this one with a finance/accounting background – and subsequently another shift in the power of the various silos of the organization. As you can easily guess by the previous statement, this time it was finance/accounting at the centre.

We all have strengths and weaknesses. There are aspects of whatever business we are in, that we are more comfortable with than we are with others – largely dependent on our education and previous experience. Each of the leaders of this company allowed the areas that they were most comfortable with, to become the centre of the organization. I believe that this illustrates the lack of humility in these leaders to do what was right for the organization rather than structure the entire company around their areas of competence.

The shift to what I will call "accounting", buried the organization in metrics (business buzzword for measurements) and bureaucracy. Let me first clarify that I do not have anything against accounting or accountants. I once heard a university professor - an accountant himself - say, "Part of the education process for an accountant is to have his or her personality removed" – but I think he was probably joking. There are those in this world that love numbers and formulas and spreadsheets, I am just not one of them.

It is impossible to run a business without good solid accounting, budgeting, financial planning and measurements. Measuring results and making decisions based on what the numbers are telling us is vital to an organizations performance. However, when all of the previously mentioned becomes the centre and core of the business, and your business is not an accounting firm, it becomes a major problem. When I use the word "accountants", I am referring to those that make decisions purely on numbers. It could be finance, planning or accounting. It could be someone that has no formal education in accounting but is employed to work numbers in some way, shape or form - essentially, those that are trained or conditioned to look no further than a spreadsheet and the data on the spreadsheet to make decisions. We should trust the "accountants" and call upon their expertise to help make decisions for the direction of the company, but there are other factors that always need to be considered.

FINANCIAL ASSORTMENT PLANNING

In the time when "The Company" experienced success, financial assortment planning (determining the merchandise assortment that the business will carry) was simplistic and only few results were measured in any major way.

Store managers themselves had a great deal of flexibility into the assortments and quantities of merchandise that they were able to pull into their stores, allowing them to meet their customer and market needs effectively. Canada is very large geographically with every different economic sector, working class, weather type, and ethnic community you can think of. It could be snowing in Montreal with temperatures below minus 20 degrees celsius at the same time that the flowers are blooming in Vancouver. The white-collar worker in Toronto makes much different purchasing decisions than the farmer in rural Saskatchewan. The only possible method to be effectively relevant to the customer in each market is to give the local store manager the ability to massage their assortments and quantity of the buy. Again, in the time that "The Company" was successful, the store manager had this ability and control. However, it was completely - and I mean completely - taken away. All decisions on the type of merchandise carried, and the quantity thereof transferred initially to the buyers, and finally to the "accountants". Here are some examples of the outcomes of that decision:

- A buyer situated in southern Ontario – who has never travelled outside of his or her home province - distributed winter goods similarly across the country regardless of the weather patterns.

    Result: Vancouver (which rarely receives any snow – but

gets rain continuously in the winter months) was overwhelmed with winter boots, coats and accessories but ran out of umbrellas while the prairie provinces (which maintain a heavy snow pack from Oct – March with no rain) ran out of the winter goods and were overwhelmed with umbrellas that they rarely sold.

- Merchandise allocations were determined based purely on the numbers. Each year's buy on any particular item was based entirely on the previous year's sales regardless of market trends, weather patterns and specific local variations – all of which could have had a dramatic impact on the previous year's results.

Result: The buy was usually too high or too low causing stores to have to deal with either excess inventories or problem shortfalls in supply. Both of which have an impact on customer satisfaction and company profitability.

- Merchandise assortments were determined based purely on the numbers at the national level. It did not matter if certain assortments sold more effectively in some areas vs. others. If the numbers were not great enough nationally – the assortment was eliminated.

Result: Stores were not able to satisfy the needs of their local customer. Specific examples would be the requirement of some communities to use blue garbage bags for recyclable trash, while others require clear or do not have any program and satisfying the needs of local ethnic groups was impossible.

I realize that the above examples sound overly simplistic, and it is hard to imagine that a large organization could completely overlook and miss basic straight forward concepts like these, but that is the outcome of years of a build-up of stifling bureaucracy and the over complication of the simple-stuff. Only recently, after 15 years has "The Company" with another change in leadership, figured out that it needs to put some decision-making ability back into the hands to those that are closest to the customer. However, the bureaucracy machine that has been built in this company is proving to be a formidable challenge in doing that. Systems that have been built with no ability to accept exceptions or manipulation have to be either thrown out altogether or substantially altered. The greater problem is that of an entire generation of store managers that have been trained to be execution specialists (do what you are told without thinking). The business experience of the former generation of managers was not transferred during the 15-year era of declining results. It is surprisingly difficult to get people who have been conditioned to "do" and not "think" to change – especially when the system keeps re-enforcing the old message.

MEASURING RESULTS

During the prosperous years, the only result that was measured with any degree of intensity was sales (revenue). That was the focus. It used to be a common saying in this company that "sales cover a multitude of sins" – meaning that if your sales were good you did not have to worry about anything else that you may not be doing well. And this was the way it was; if your sales were good, you could do no wrong – nothing else seemed to matter that much. If your sales were not good, the focus and attention that you received was intense and severe. This was the way that it worked during the prosperous times, which would indicate that this focus just might have been sound.

When the "accountants" began to take over, the measurements – or metrics, began to increase and never stopped increasing. Someone took the saying "What gets measured – gets done (or improves)" and applied it to everything with the hope that everything would improve. What's that?... you have a particular result that is not where you want it to be – just put some metrics to it – create a spreadsheet or better yet – a dashboard, and the results will improve. (Results can be shown in a myriad of ways; one of them is the dashboard. This is a strong visual report that rolls all of the results up to a summary type display similar to what you have in your car. It is meant to show at a glance where potential problems might exist within subcategories of results.)

Everything got measured and everything that was measured was reported. Internal websites were set up with multiple hierarchies and levels of reports. Every division had to have their own special page on the website with their own series of reports. The existence of reporting created an implied expectation that the issue being measured was important. The problem: Because everything was measured – everything was important. In this company, one could spend 100% of their time reading and analysing the reports available to them and end up spending zero time doing anything to change the actual results that were being reported. In fact, this is what happened. The entire organization became paralysed by reports, spreadsheets and metrics. Countless hours are wasted everyday responding, justifying and explaining why a certain result is the way it is rather than working to improve the result. From a survival standpoint, people learned to manipulate the results being reported to avoid attention simply because there is no way you can fix every result when you are measuring everything.

The greatest consequence was a frequent penchant for an entire organization to put a greater focus on issues that had minimal or no impact to the bottom line vs. issues that had a critical impact on the bottom line. Top line sales declined every year during the 15 years that this book is based on. The all-important metric of "sales results" became lost in the myriad of other comparably meaningless metrics – those fringe metrics that have almost no impact on customer service or company profitability.

Spreadsheets and software reporting programs became the focus of "The Company". The results were not good and the thinking was, if only it could measure more - the results would improve. I suppose from an accountant's perspective – this seems to make sense. I watched "The Company" grow up from archaic simple reporting mechanisms to extremely complex integrated software reporting tools. At first, the organization – including me - applauded the new and growing complex reporting systems. It is a fact that if you put a frog in water and slowly increase the heat until the water boils – the frog will not jump out and will perish. We were just like the frog being boiled in the water. The metrics, spreadsheets and reporting tools continued to grow and before we realized it, we were overcome.

"The Company" probably should have become a "software/reporting system development company" as they really became very good at it. In fact, this focus became so profound; the use of a particular new software-reporting program was specifically called out as performance review criteria for my role and others in the organization. What this means is; one of my job responsibilities was to effectively use a software reporting program, and I was going to be evaluated on that effective use of the software program. Remember, I was a district manager overseeing a group of retail stores and responsible for the execution of the company strategy and maximization of the profit of my group of stores. I was not an accountant, an analyst, or an "information technology" specialist. It was the same as asking an automobile repairperson to make sure they use one specific tool very effectively – above all their other tools. If they can repair the car without using that one tool – does it really matter in the end? An organization truly loses their way when the tools of the trade become <u>more</u> important than the reason that they exist.

Focus on the Most Important Results

There is a finite limit to what an individual is able to focus on effectively. Since companies and organizations are made up of individuals, the principle is the same for them. This limit is much less than what is normally accepted. Take the subject of multitasking as an example. There are those that claim they have the ability to multitask or the ability to do (perform/carryout) more than one mental task at a time. Some common examples: Watching television and reading or doing homework; driving and talking on the cell phone and/or putting on makeup; reading and listening to someone talking or the most common; listening and talking. Despite what you might think, you cannot do both of these at exactly the same time. One of the activities suffers at the expense of the other.

It is impossible to carryout two voluntary mental activities at the same time.

I expect that a large number reading that statement vehemently disagree – especially females. I do not want to be perceived as sexist here – there are certainly many men in this camp, but the female gender generally makes the claim that they are somehow gifted with the ability to multitask and so deceive themselves by constantly attempting to do it. The fact is that your mind can switch its focus back and forth between tasks – and do it rapidly, but it cannot focus on two tasks at exactly the same time. Moreover, when one considers him or herself to be multitasking, they are in reality rapidly switching their focus between the two, three or more tasks that they are trying to do. Because of this switching, their productivity and effectiveness is decreased. The reason for this reduced productivity is the continual need to refocus on each task as you switch. When we are interrupted while reading, it takes a few seconds to find our place again – both on the page and mentally – before we can resume reading. Sure, it is only a very brief period of time and in the case of watching TV and reading at the same time - it may only be a fraction of a second for each switch of focus. But any benefit that you may get from either of the activities, (assuming that you were watching a television program that could provide benefit), will be decreased, and it will ultimately take you more time to do both tasks at the same time than it would have to do each separately. Think about this the next time you consider yourself to be multitasking.

If we understand that we can only truly focus on one thing at a time, and agree that an organization made up of people, can only focus on more than one thing, by switching the focus, we realize that there needs to be a limit on that which is put on the priority list. The larger the list of results that an organization is forced to focus on - and the subsequent switching back and forth between them– the less productive and the less effective the organization becomes. The amount of specific results metrics that an organization can focus on depends on the size, ability and experience of that organization and it is relatively easy to determine. What you work on, works – what you stop working on, stops working. If the list of priorities or issues that you expect focus on, grows to the point where some of those issues stop working – you have likely exceeded your organizations threshold.

Very careful consideration must be given to what is measured. If you are measuring something, it is a focus – regardless of whether you intended it to be or not. Some leaders think that their team has this magical ability to discern what is really important regardless of how many activities or results are being measured. Please understand that if it is being measured, someone in your organization is going to latch on to it and drive it. Once others start to see the positive results they will also start driving it primarily out of shame. Visionless leaders will see this and actually encourage it further, without noticing and understanding that the focus has been shifted from what should be the priorities – those that provide the best payback. Those individuals on the team that can see the problem with all of this, must either; relent and conform – do things right; or do the right thing and just focus on the true priority metrics. This is a risk, it could prove successful in leading up (influencing those that you report to) and help guide the company back on course - or - it could be career ending.

Being aware of your organization's ability and threshold for focus, you will need to prioritize what it is that you expect to be focused on. The results that you focus on - that you put the most time, energy and effort against – should provide maximum payback. Payback should align very closely to pursuit of your company's mission statement and bottom line profitability.

When "The Company" initially started down the road of increased metrics and measurements, they began on the right track. Much time and effort was put into sifting through all of the data available to come up with the most important metrics. It was an endeavour to determine scientifically those metrics or results that truly had an impact on the bottom line vs. those that did not – regardless of what the conventional wisdom was. A final list of eight Key Performance Indicators (KPI) was produced. These were the eight metrics that if improved upon would have the greatest influence on the profitability of the company. There were many revelations in this process in that most of the metrics that were initially thought to be important did not have anywhere near the impact as some others. For example, top lines sales growth is an important metric. However, instead of measuring it as a comparison to last year, it was determined that is was more accurate and effective to measure "sales per selling square foot". These KPI metrics were very specific to this company. KPI metrics would never be the same in any two organizations.

Understanding the science of the numbers behind the conclusion of the KPI's (the great work of the "accountants"), it was easy to buy into the fact that if we focus on driving these, we will get better. The irony in "The Company's" case is that it never moved to just focusing on these eight KPIs. They (KPIs) were just the start of the myriad of metrics and measurements that were put on the list to drive and eventually got lost in the shuffle.

Every organization must determine what their list of KPIs is going to be. As mentioned, the list will be as different as the fingerprints between people as it will be between companies and organizations. It is my opinion that every effort should be made to make this list as short as possible – fewer than four if possible. When you get proficient at the list you do have, you can always consider adding more if it makes sense to do so.

Once you have determined the metrics that make up your KPIs, you will then need to decide what you will not measure. It seems logical and straightforward that if something is not on the KPI list, it would not get measured. This is deceiving. It needs to be made clear across the organization what will be measured and what will not be measured. A "stop doing" list should be made to eliminate those issues that do not fall in the

KPIs. It is likely that you will have to revisit this "stop doing" list frequently to add those measurements that have crept in from well meaning people. If we are serious about keeping the organization focused, and we trust the "accountants" assessment of what should be measured (KPIs), why would we deviate and add additional metrics?

The word "key" in KPI means that you will select those metrics that provide the most payback to your organization. Choosing a metric that will make only a small difference to achieving your goals is not only a waste of time and effort but destroys focus and clarity.

Let us look at a real life example from "The Company". The subject of "credit" explained in chapter two. Not surprisingly, one of the eight KPIs for "The Company" was "credit blend" (the percentage of total sales that were put onto "The Company's" credit cards). It was scientifically determined that focus on increasing the credit blend would have the largest impact on the bottom line. Unfortunately, there was more focus placed on signing up new accounts than there was on "credit blend". Not a change of focus, but another focus or an added focus. With the benefits that a customer could receive by signing up for a new account, it was easy to drive this number up. However, when customers are signing up for a new account every time they shop in order to receive those extra benefits, it becomes obvious that those new accounts will have no positive impact on the bottom line. It was a metric that could be made to look good by those industrious "yes" people. In fact this pursuit did more to increase costs (cost of benefits given to customers for signing up) than it did to drive credit profits. In also took the focus away from the KPI of credit blend – that metric which would have the most payback and one that could not be fictitiously enhanced by any means. In this case, "The Company" did not trust the "accountants" and serves as a prime example, of the many, where additional metrics were added without careful thought and analysis.

THE POINT IS TO TAKE ACTION

It is common sense to take a method and try it. If it fails, admit it frankly and try another. But above all, try something.
Franklin D. Roosevelt:

There are those things we like to do and those that we would rather not do, which match accordingly to our strengths and weaknesses. Repeating what I wrote earlier, there are those that like to work with numbers; that like to create spreadsheets and reports. They derive the same pleasure from this that an artist gets from painting or sculpting. This is just fine as long as there are limits placed on the output. I have found that "report makers", left unrestricted, will continue indefinitely to make spreadsheets and find new metrics to report on. I come from an organization where there is more excitement about the structure and content of a report rather than on the message, which the report conveys. We need to be concerned when we hear comments such as "we are very proud of this particular report". Unless your company's business is to make reports, the focus of any report must be the results it measures.

When it comes to getting things done, we need fewer architects and more bricklayers.
Colleen C. Barrett:

I have worked in a company that is paralysed by the sheer amount of metrics reporting, as illustrated at the start of this chapter. I have watched endless lists of terrible results reported for months and in some cases, years, with little or no action taken to improve them. "The Company" was so busy and over whelmed with reading, analysing and explaining the results, that little or nothing was ever done to change them. The leaders convince themselves that they are doing the right thing based on the "yes" people. There are always those that pop up that seem to have a superhuman ability to make most of the "fringe metrics" look good. The "fringe metrics" are those that can be manipulated and are never found in the list of KPIs. When overall results are not good, wayward leaders will latch on to anything that shows a positive trend.

How many legs does a dog have if you call the tail a leg? Four; calling a tail a leg doesn't make it a leg.
Abraham Lincoln:

The difference between those that are true high performers and those that are "yes" people is the way that the results on these "fringe metrics" are achieved. "Yes" people are motivated to find a way to please vs. doing what is right – to find a way to make things look good. In the pursuit of making things look good – they are prepared to do anything - including putting their integrity into question. It is easy to find them out – just look a little deeper and you will easily be able to sift the high performers from the "yes" people. However, weak leaders choose to put their hands over their ears and close their eyes. It is easier and much less work for them to think that; if some are doing it – all should be able to.

There are basically two types of people. People who accomplish things, and people who claim to have accomplished things. The first group is less crowded.
Mark Twain:

High performing individuals intuitively understand the difference between the "fringe metrics" and the results that will deliver the bottom line. They are able to sift between those that are linked to positive results against the organizations goals and those that are time-wasters and focus-diverters.

When you get to the right list of objectives that you are going to measure - the KPIs - and stop every other time wasting report and metric, you can start to enhance the results you are looking at. This, after all, is the point of the metrics in the first place. Spend your time on developing and executing plans of action to influence those key metrics that you are measuring in a positive way. In fact, there is not much point in creating any new report on those key metrics if you have done nothing to improve them. If you have not done anything - not taken steps to change the results - they are not going to mysteriously and magically improve. Moreover, if you have not taken any action, do not wait for next months report; it is not likely going to be any different from the one you have in your possession today. Stop hoping for magic to happen.

IT IS NOT JUST ABOUT NUMBERS

Inventories can be managed, but people must be led.
H. Ross Perot

When your organization began, it did not evolve out of a financial formula, but rather an idea, concept or service to meet the needs or solve the problems of your customers. Certainly, financial planning was necessary to start, fund and properly manage your organization, but it was not the root. In "The Company", we can see that they failed to put first things first and put the financials ahead of the customer. This blurred their vision so much so, that those simple and very basic decisions such as putting winter goods in the prairie provinces and umbrellas in the rain stricken Vancouver could no longer be made. Financial planning is critical, and must be utilized to maximize inventory productivity and sales results. However, as you saw in the examples provided, a reliance exclusively on the financial numbers caused both inventory productivity and sales results to decline. It limited and restricted "The Company's" ability to serve their customers adequately by providing them with the right goods at the right time to meet their needs. This exclusive reliance on the numbers is part of the reason for "The Company's" failure to post a positive sales increase in the past 15 years.

Fortunately, for all us (who are not "accountants"), the numbers, the math, the computers and formulas will never replace the power of the human mind and its ingenuity. All those previous things help individuals and teams of individuals (organizations) become more effective and productive, but when we decide to exclude and eliminate good critical thinking, and experience in our decision-making – we will fail. When you call upon the expertise of everyone in your organization, you can have both solid financial planning and customer satisfaction. As Jim Collins states in his book, "Built to Last" – "It's the tyranny of the 'or' - the genius of the 'and'".[1]

It is the responsibility of the leadership of any organization to keep this in perspective. If the leadership leaves the decision of - what is going to be measured - up to the "spreadsheet makers", the organization will likely become buried, overwhelmed and ineffective.

―――――

It is true that "What gets measured – gets done". It is also true that too much of a good thing is not good for you and can make you sick – or in this case your organization. There are limits to what an organization can effectively focus on. When you begin to push the envelope of those limits, it is not more that you will get – but less. The organization will not push harder, work harder and achieve more. Instead, they will become confused, unfocused and undisciplined.

Speaking from the perspective of the middle of an organization, I can tell you that they will also become demoralized. Those that are in place to directly serve the customer but are not given the tools with which to do that on a continual basis, do not find much satisfaction in their jobs.

What it means to "win" must be clear to everyone. In other words, what is that one result that defines if we have done well? Sports teams never get confused on the definition of the "win". A hockey coach certainly uses and works on issues such as face off wins, penalty minutes, etc. in an attempt to improve overall performance. However, no hockey team gets depressed in the dressing room after a game win over issues like less than ideal face off wins, and scoreless power-plays.

We can use or spin results (numbers) in any way that we choose. They can be used to build up or beat up. Groups and individuals become masters at making themselves look good by spinning results in their favour. Continued focus on your purpose and vision will help to detect when results are being spun in someone's favour.

If you currently belong to or oversee a company that has typically been very focused on what they will measure, and spends the greater portion of their time in working to improve upon those results, I suspect that your organization is one that is currently thriving. Based on the performance and results of "The Company" I would suggest that you use the principles mentioned in this chapter to ensure that you remain on track in this area.

It is of course the role of the leader to put the necessary limits in this area. Strong leaders rely on the skills and experience of those around them. They are not too proud to recognize and admit that they are not experts in every area and they certainly do not change the world to make themselves look more competent and comfortable. They consult and listen and look for the "and" instead of the "or". However, in the end they need to make the final decisions and stand by their decisions. If they do not make the decisions and decide what will and what will not be measured, everyone else will.

However, everyone else has their own agenda and the company will be directed by a hundred individuals in one hundred different directions.

Strong leaders understand that there are always people that would rather work by illusion rather than by reality, and they do not demoralize an organization by recognizing and rewarding it. In the end, it is only "reality" that is going to covert down to the bottom line and allow your organization to achieve its purpose.

Let us take things as we find them: let us not attempt to distort them into what they are not. We cannot make facts. All our wishing cannot change them. We must use them.

John Henry Cardinal Newman (1801 - 1890)

Chapter Six

YOU ARE ONLY AS GOOD AS YOUR WEAKEST LINK

"THE COMPANY"

"The Company" is an extremely fragile organization. The links in its organizational chain have been neglected for years and left to rust and deteriorate. Worse still, is that many of these links are not even hooked securely to the others due to the empire and silo building described earlier. Imagine a long stretch of decayed and cracked chain with many of the links open at their joints. If one is to shake the chain even slightly, those open joints shake loose and the entire chain falls limp in your hands. If a leader manages to pull the chain in one direction without jostling it too much, he or she may be able to make some progress, but if that pull becomes forceful and significant enough to move the organization, any one of the many weak links snap causing the chain to fall limp and the organization fails to move.

A leader should be able to pull an organization in the direction they choose without problem – without the chain continuously breaking. However, when it is discovered that this is not possible, a leader must shift his or her focus to chain itself. In other words, shift their focus to restoring and rebuilding the organization, and when a leader has to spend the majority of their time on "fixing the chain", rather than focusing on their vision, there can be some criticism from those that the leader reports to. After all, the leader was put in place to move "The Company" forward. There will not be much patience for a long extended period of repair and "organization building". Therefore, each leader in "The Company" had a decision to make. Stop and repair the ship – or push forward regardless of the condition of the ship and try to repair as we go. I regret to say that each of the leaders in the 15 years of declining results chose the second option – push forward regardless and try to repair on the fly. It is very difficult to win the battle when the lion's share of your crew is working at just trying to keep the ship running with overlapping duct tape and band-aids.

The strong links in "The Company" would often show signs of brilliance and greatness in the form of superior strategies and plans that had the potential to propel the company into abundant success. All too often, these plans would hit the weak link in the chain and fall to the floor of failure.

- Marketing events destroyed by the inability of distribution to get the goods to the stores.

- Superior buys that are not even seen by the customer until the end of the season because the store did not get it out of the stockrooms.
- Missed sales due to breakdowns in the systems.
- Missed opportunities due to poor and non-existent lines of communication between functional groups.

This was a constant source of frustration for everyone in the organization. There is nothing more de-motivating to a group or an individual than to see your great ideas fail due to another person or group's failure to execute.

I am not naïve enough to think that these types of problems do not occur in other organizations, but I am saying that in "The Company", the ideas and strategies fail the majority of the time - hence its inability to find success in the past 15 years.

The most obvious and detrimental example would be the previously mentioned inability to have the merchandise to sell to the customer or poor "in-stock" as it is called in the business. There is little doubt that "The Company" has the poorest "in-stock" record in the nation. The sad fact is that while everyone knows it, little has been done about it. The customer certainly knows it and has responded appropriately as evidenced by "The Company's" sales results. Vendors (distributors and manufacturers of the products that are sold in stores) know it and can easily make comparisons to other retailers that they supply. Everyone inside the organization both know and feel this problem intimately everyday. This problem is a common source of frustration for everyone; the customer because they cannot fill their shopping list when they come in; the vendor due to less sales than the existing potential; and "The Company" due to the failure of almost every initiative to improve results. Nothing will compensate for a lack in the merchandise to sell. Despite this, and now going beyond 15 years, the problem remains.

Imagine a DVD rental outlet without sufficient DVDs to rent, an asphalt paving company without a sufficient supply of asphalt, a pipeline company with a lack in available pipes to install. "The Company" is a retail chain without sufficient merchandise to sell.

The statements made in the preceding two paragraphs must seem almost unbelievable. I imagine you the reader doubting that a problem like this, known by everyone to be the main source of the poor results, would be ignored. For Canadians: If I were to divulge the name of "The Company", current and especially former customers and vendors would overwhelmingly be able to confirm this. Any employee of the company reading this, or any part of this book for that matter, have already guessed that this is their company, because of the unmistakable descriptions of problems that exist. That is just how obvious this problem is. I also expect that anyone working in a large – broken - organization would be able to draw some comparisons to their own experiences.

This is a very poignant example of what happens when leaders choose to ignore the brutal reality that is in front of them. The "yes people" also play a major role in this problem.

There are primarily three reasons that have caused the leadership of "The Company" to, for the most part, ignore this problem.

1. There are the reports that have been spun to show "in-stock" rates that are better than reality (previously

mentioned in chapter 4). These reports, which are created only to protect and exalt those that create them, do not represent reality. Sadly, they are believed to be accurate.

2. Some stores actually do have better "in-stock" rates – those that are closest to the distribution centres. This better "in-stock" is simply a consequence of logistics. If a store can be replenished within 24 hours because of their proximity to the centre that supplies the merchandise – it provides that location with a distinct advantage over one that takes two weeks or more to replenish.

3. Beyond the reports and metrics – which do not help the customer – one can observe the "in-stock" on the selling floor – good or bad. Many of the "yes people" create an illusion for the leadership of the company by "faking" the "in-stock" (incidentally the word "faking" is actually used to describe this practice). This is done by spreading out the merchandise that is "in-stock" over the spaces of the items that are sold out. Visually, at a distance, it looks full – the store looks like it is 100% "in-stock". Certainly, a closer look would reveal the "fake" and of course, this does nothing to help the customer (more of the same does not fill the shopping list). Leaders that do not look for the truth do not take that "closer look". In fact, this illusion usually caused the leader to take the approach of, "if this store can be 100% 'in-stock' – all stores should be able to accomplish the same result".

The leaders of "The Company" chose to ignore the weak

links of the chain. If they were to acknowledge the problems, they would be obligated to work to correct them – to allocate resources to them. Moreover, as mentioned, allocating resources to these seemingly trivial problems not only takes away from future progress, but also has the potential to make the leader look incompetent. Using the example given above, imagine a leader having to report that they have spent the majority of their time working on and correcting something as basic as "in-stock" in a retail company. It is much easier to pretend that they [the problems] are not there in order to avoid the guilt of not allocating time and resources to solve them. A leader that discourages critical thinking and honesty creates an environment that makes it very easy for him or her to ignore these kinds of problems. This is precisely how it works in "The Company". Everyone loses when this happens, including those leaders who were all eventually removed from their post.

❋❋❋❋❋❋❋❋

WEAK LINKS

Military leaders understand weak links better than any of us. Perhaps this is because of the consequence of choosing to ignore them, which is simply, defeat. In war, defeat means lost lives, lost territory and freedoms. For this reason, military leaders are always concerned about the weakest link – their own and the enemies. One does not attack an enemy on their strongest front. It is most advantageous to attack them at their weakest point. This assures the best chance of victory. It does not matter how strong or well trained an army is. It does not matter how much more or superior equipment that it has. If you are not watching and working to improve your weakest link, you are vulnerable to defeat. Think about the events of September 11, 2001. The greatest superpower on the planet was attacked on their own soil with their own passenger airlines. The enemy will not attack with conventional weapons and tactics – they know that they cannot win in this type of attack. Instead, they will continue to seek those areas that are the easiest to attack – the weakest links.

Similar to wars – business is won and lost on "weakest links". Companies do not view their competition to find out where they are the strongest and then try to exploit them on that. No, they look for the areas that are most vulnerable and then build strategies to take advantage of them in those areas.

It is the same in all aspects of life. An engineer must be constantly aware of the weak links. An insufficient quantity or type of bolts – one of the smallest components - can bring and entire skyscraper down to a pile of rubble. The best-designed automobile can be rendered useless if a small part in the drive train fails. A triathelete understands that it is their worst segment of the three-part marathon that can prevent him or her from winning.

Perhaps the most vivid example of the consequences of weak links is that of the tragic Space Shuttle Challenger disaster. On January 28, 1986, the Challenger broke apart 73 seconds into its flight leading to the deaths of its seven crewmembers. This tragic disaster was eventually found to be the result of a single O-ring that failed to seal on the shuttle's right solid rocket booster.[1]

DIFFERENCE BETWEEN "WEAK LINKS" AND "WEAKNESSES"

Wisdom (and of course Markus Buckingham – author of Go Put Your Strengths to Work, as well as other books[2]) has taught me that I should focus on my greatest personal strengths and not on my weaknesses, which may sound contradictory after reading the above paragraphs. Personal strengths and weaknesses define what you do well and that which you do not do well. Surprisingly, most people cannot even truly define what these are in themselves. Focusing on those areas that you are good at and really like – your strengths – will have exponential dividends and will bring you the most success in life. I have also come to the conclusion, from personal experience and the wisdom of others, that you really cannot fix your own personal weaknesses. You can potentially improve on them with some focus but they will always be a weakness.

The same is not true with organizations. Weaknesses can be overcome. The difference is that in organizations we are not dealing with only one personality but with groups of people. Weak links are those weak points in an organization that set the limit of what the organization can accomplish and they [weak links] can be easily strengthened with focus. If any link in a chain (an organization) breaks, the chain (organization) becomes useless. Weak links are the limits that an organization has within it. For example if we use an electrical circuit as an analogy, it is the fuse of that circuit that is the weakest link. The fuse is purposely put in place to protect the circuit from damage if there is an overload. Without the fuse, an overload could cause one or more of the components of the circuit to overheat and cause a fire. Therefore, the fuse is for safety in an electrical circuit. When the fuse blows or cuts the power – the circuit immediately becomes dead. The fuse in an organization is also the weakest link. When it blows, the entire organization loses power. In an electrical circuit, we do want the power to be cut in the event of an overload or extra stress and pressure, but we do not what this to happen in an organization. Most of us have experienced the devastating drain of energy that a blown link has on an entire organization – it really does take the wind out of the sails. This is how the weakest link puts limits on the entire organization. They [weak links] have the potential to stop the entire organization in an instant, and ignoring them will always have negative consequences.

THE CREAM ALWAYS RISES TO THE TOP

High performing individuals will always stand out among their peers. Groups or divisions that are led by, or have high performing people within them, will usually become the strongest links in the chain of the organization. Your company may have strong individuals leading every division, and each division may have an abundance of high performing people. This makes the entire organization strong, but regardless of how many high performers you have and how many of your divisions are led by them; there will still be strong and weak links. Your chain may be stronger overall – but there will still be a limit to the overall strength of the chain. The stronger you can make it – the more effectively you will be able to execute and compete and the more successful your organization will be. It is important to understand what your limits are and not to attempt to pull your organization beyond them. Stretching a chain is good and like exercise to the body, it helps to build it stronger. However, stretch a chain to its breaking point and the energy will be suddenly cut off to your organization just like a torn tendon will stop an athlete in their tracks.

I never cease being dumbfounded by the unbelievable things people believe.
Leo Rosten (1908 -)

The approach that "The Company" took was to assume and expect that every link was automatically as strong as the strongest link. The leaders deceived themselves by thinking that if a handful can do it – then everyone should be able to. Certainly if the majority of your organization can do what you expect, then it is obvious that the problem lies with the performance in the minority – those that cannot do what you expect. However, if only 10% are able to achieve the goals and expectations that you the leader have established, we are most likely talking about the strongest performers. Moreover, assuming that everyone should automatically rise to that level is illusionary. The other element that must be considered is that of the "smoke and mirrors" and "politics" of the "yes people". Leaders must always pay careful attention to make sure that the top results are true and not someone's attempt at personal significance and glory by hiding the facts.

Benchmarking and challenging the organization to strive for the results of the best 10% is good, but expecting that they are already there is a problem that will cause the chain to continually break.

This brings with it a dilemma of sorts. If you manage to the strongest link (performers) and expect all to achieve the same – your organization will suffer from breakdowns on a regular basis as outlined in this chapter. On the other hand, if you manage to the weakest link, you will stifle your strongest links and completely limit your organizations possibilities. There needs to be a balance. You need to challenge your best people and strongest divisions to become better in order to keep them engaged. You also need to give them hope by making it clear that you are doing everything possible to strengthen those weaker links – the parts of the organization that has been limiting them (the stronger). Then do what you say – work at strengthening the weaker links and challenge them to rise to the level of the best.

WHERE TO START

We identify the weaker links by purposefully looking for them – seeking them out. Similar to the airline pilot that does a walk around their aircraft before every flight, we must do a virtual walk around our organization. We do not want to discover our weakest links by having them break during operation any more than the airline pilot wants to find them during a flight. When we seek with a genuine desire to see the truth, we will find them. Some leaders seem to think that acknowledging a weak link will validate it and make it real and that if they ignore it and instead project an expectation that it is really a strong link, it will magically become a strong link. In "The Company", this was displayed in the continuous suggestion by the leadership that the "in-stock", based on the reports, was as good as the industry average. I believe that this comes from the feeling that if they acknowledge a problem it somehow becomes acceptance of that problem and they believe that acceptance will mean that they are ok with it. Therefore, the thinking is; if I the leader, acknowledge that our "in-stock" rate is dismal, everyone will relax because now that I understand the problem, there is no longer any pressure. In reality, the opposite is true. The alcoholic or drug addict will never get clean until they acknowledge that they truly do have a problem. It is only then that they can start taking positive steps toward recovery. In an organization; when the problems are identified and acknowledged, the pressure - or better described as focus - changes from trying to pretend, to actually taking steps to correct. Pretending that there is not a problem and believing that it will somehow improve or solve itself is not leadership. This is denial and a cowardly approach at leading a team.

Therefore, if we look within our organizations, actively encourage and seek the truth, we will be able to identify the weak links easily and quickly. Depending on the organization, this [actively seeking out the problems] may require a complete and sudden 180-degree change in approach. Depending on the leader, it may require a significant *coming down in stature* and significant *rise up in humility*. For some to say, "I want to hear about our problems", is just about as hard for them to say, "I am not perfect".

However, when this pursuit of reality finally takes place, the problems will be surprisingly easy to identify and solve. It is likely that the answers have been there all along. It is only because there was never an effort to seek the problems in the past that the answers were hidden. Looking at past experience is usually a good place to start to identify those weak links. Where has your company broken down in the past? What areas of the organization have caused you to fail in the past? If your organization is anything like "The Company", the problems may be rooted in years of denial and it may take a little more time and focus to get at the strengthening of those weak links. In either event, all work toward this end will have a reward in the increased strength of the chain – your organization.

ooooo

Nothing in the world is more dangerous than sincere ignorance and conscientious stupidity.
Martin Luther King, Jr.

Denial and forced ignorance of our problems – our weak links – will not make them any less real. Although we would like them to, they are not likely going to magically correct themselves or disappear. This is really about a "strive for excellence". We all want to do a great job. No one strives for mediocrity and failure. Those weak links are a source of frustration for everyone and prevent the individual and the organization from achieving excellence. If left unchecked, these weak links will suck the hope out of the entire organization. "The Company" is an organization without hope. If you were to interview a cross section of those that work in the organization, you would quickly find an atmosphere of despair. There is little hope and expectation for the future. This is the result of years of repeated breaks in a chain full of un-addressed weak links.

Every worthy endeavour takes planning and preparation. Those that embark on climbing to the tallest point on the earth – Mount Everest – spend months and years in the planning process before they even arrive at the mountain. Their very lives depend upon it. When you are climbing a mountain, i.e.: Mount Everest, a break in any link of the chain, will almost guarantee an unsuccessful attempt and you will be fortunate if you do get back down the mountain with your life. Continuous neglect of your equipment when skydiving will likely get your spouse a payout on your life insurance.

If adherence to the equipment, the parts, and the components is so obviously important, why do some choose to neglect it? It is simply a failure in leadership.

Your company is only as good as its weakest link. Identify it. Strengthen it. Then continue to repeat that process on the next weakest link – forever.

> *There is nothing so useless as doing efficiently that which should not be done at all.*
>
> *Peter F. Drucker*

Chapter Seven

SIMPLIFY

A MODERN DAY PARABLE

A Japanese company (Toyota) and an American company (Ford Motor Company) decided to have a canoe race on the Missouri River. Both teams practiced long and hard to reach their peak performance before the race. On the big day, the Japanese won by a mile.

The Americans, very discouraged and depressed, decided to investigate the reason for the crushing defeat. A management team made up of senior management was formed to investigate and recommend appropriate action. Their conclusion was the Japanese had eight people rowing and one person steering, while the American team had eight people steering and one person rowing. Feeling a deeper study was in order, American management hired a consulting company and paid them a large amount of money for a second opinion. They advised, of course, that too many people were steering the boat, while not enough people were rowing.

Not sure of how to utilize that information, but wanting to prevent another loss to the Japanese, the rowing team's management structure was totally reorganized to four steering supervisors, three area steering superintendents and one assistant superintendent steering manager. They also implemented a new performance system that would give the one person rowing the boat greater incentive to work harder. It was called the 'Rowing Team Quality First Program,' with meetings, dinners, and free pens for the rower. There was discussion of getting new paddles, canoes and other equipment, extra vacation days for practices and bonuses. The next year the Japanese won by two miles.

Humiliated, the American management laid off the rower for poor performance, halted development of a new canoe, sold the paddles, and cancelled all capital investments for new equipment. The money saved was distributed to the Senior Executives as bonuses and the next year's racing team was out-sourced to India. Sadly, THE END.

Here's something else to think about: Ford has spent the last thirty years moving all its factories out of the US, claiming they can't make money paying American wages. Toyota has spent the last thirty years building more than a dozen plants inside the US. The last quarter's results: Toyota makes four billion in profits while Ford racked up nine billion in losses. Ford folks are still scratching their heads.[1]

"THE COMPANY"

Let's say that you purchased a new toaster – the thing that makes your bread warm and crusty and causes it to be a little more rigid than just plain old bread. This appliance quickly transforms ordinary bread into a fragrant new entity that is a delight to enjoy with anyone of your favourite jams or spreads. Imagine that you received an operating manual with your new toaster, except that this manual is in a separate box because it is 360 pages long. It goes into detail on the origin, history and evolution of the toaster. The manual explains how the toaster is built, how many were manufactured and when your particular model was manufactured. It contains pictures of the individuals that work in the factory that manufactured the toaster. The manual gives detailed illustration on how to set up the toaster, where to place it on the counter, how to use it and even what to do with the toaster when it finally comes to the end of its life. When it comes to toasters, there is nothing that is not included in this manual.

Would you read this manual? Perhaps if you have never operated or seen a toaster, bread or experienced the wonders of electricity. However, if you are like the majority that live in North America - you have used a toaster at least once in your lifetime and would probably not take the time to read this manual. You likely open the manual out of curiosity and wonder why the manufacturer of this appliance would send such a large manual for such a simple appliance. You would likely flip through few pages and quickly realize that this is much more information than you care to know or have time to read. You would likely put the manual down without reading or noticing the key important and relevant points of information that you probably should know about your new toaster; such as the prudent reminder not to stick a metal utensil in your toaster to remove a lodged bagel while it is plugged in to the wall receptacle. You would likely get aggravated by the amount of paper and wasted trees that were used in the production of this manual and conclude that you probably paid for the cost of that excessively large manual in the price of your toaster, continuing to develop resentment for the company that made it. Your frustration would intensify when the manufacturer begins to send out updates to your unreasonably large instruction manual, most of which are repeats of what is already in the manual. These updates are being sent because the manufacturer has discovered that one or more of their customers have not read the manual and have missed some important information; they were possibly electrocuted after sticking a metal utensil in the toaster. Your aggravation would cause that company to lose any credibility that they had with you and you would never purchase another appliance from them again.

Wow! That was a lot of detail for a toaster purchase story. I suspect that you did not need the detailed description at the beginning of what a toaster does. I expect that you read the story patiently expecting to get some revolutionary information or lesson and were disappointed when you did not. Now, try to imagine if this was real – if it really happened this way. Wouldn't this be ridiculous? This is how "The Company" operates! No exaggeration! In fact it is so close to reality, I believe anyone working in "The Company" would instantly recognize the analogy of the "toaster story" to the over complication of communication in the company. The toaster story provides an idea of the overkill of information and communication that is a constant in "The Company".

"How-to" or instruction in "The Company" is created with a mindset that the individuals who it is written for - know nothing. Each and every small detail is explained. Those things that ought to be known by someone are explained and over-explained, i.e.: explaining how a toaster works to someone that has used one previously. There are no assumptions made that someone may already know something. The paper and data download flow is overwhelming. We are not talking about the analogy of "trying to drink water out of a fire hose". That would suggest that the information is good and that those that are receiving want it. A better analogy would be like trying to find a diamond in the sand. Most of the information is unnecessary and unwanted. Some of the information is critical but is missed because it is lost in the myriad of unnecessary and often useless, excess words, facts and figures. Then since the real, good and useful information is often missed, updates and reminders are frequently sent out in an attempt to close the gaps, which results in even more communication. In the end, this company has become one that is filled with employees that pick and choose what they will read and do, creating a complete loss of credibility up, down and across the organization with the result of hit and miss execution. More communication is not necessarily better – quantity is not better than quality.

When "The Company" was successful, communication, instruction and "how-to" was very basic and high level. This was before the prolific use of email and other technology that allows large documents, instruction manuals etc. to be instantly transmitted. During the era when the "buying division" ran the organization, a new silo was put in place – called "in store marketing". This silo was created to develop and communicate what the buying division wanted the stores to do, how to do it, when to do it, etc. It was truly a top down focus – do what we tell you to do and everything will work.

Some may read this and wonder what the problem is. Shouldn't organizations communicate what is expected to be done and have those expectations met? Yes, but you do not want to suck every ounce of "think" out of your organization. Instruction needs to be appropriate for the level you are communicating to. Like the analogy of the toaster above – you do not need to explain what a toaster is and how to use it in much detail to someone who has used one before any more than you have to explain the basics of how to do one's job when they have been doing it for years. "The Company" created "doers" as a result of this detailed communication and instruction and suffocated the "thinkers". Good thinking was suppressed and stifled by the overwhelming amount of communication. If parents never teach or allow their kids to tie their own shoes, they will still be asking them to tie their shoes for them when they are 40 years old. I do not think any organization wants to deliberately eliminate good thinking and creativity.

"The Company" has only recently begun to realize the problem that they have created. The organization can no longer move, evolve and effectively compete in the marketplace. It is an organization of "obedience", waiting for the next list of instructions to execute, often missing great opportunities that are directly in front of them. "The Company" has only recently tried to push an atmosphere of entrepreneurship. I use the word "push" rather than "stimulate" on purpose. To stimulate would mean that they had created an environment to foster entrepreneurship, that is, to plant seeds in good soil and water them. "The Company" has indeed attempted to plant some good seeds for entrepreneurship and is trying their best to water them. The problem is that they have planted those seeds on the asphalt of continued detailed instruction and direction, which has prevented them from being able to take root and grow.

"The Company" would like every person in the organization to think and look for ideas that will help make the organization more relevant to the customer. This is called empowerment. Unfortunately, the massive amount of instruction has not subsided and the push for increased thinking has created more frustration than anything else - frustration in a team that sees the merit of creative thinking, wants to be entrepreneurial, but is constantly buried under the suppressing amount of direction. Ironically, they were better off in the "don't think – just do" phase because it was less frustrating. The level of dissatisfaction among those that work in "The Company" is very high at almost all levels in the hierarchy. "The Company" has traditionally paid very well in their industry at the executive level (store manager and above) and this has kept turnover to a minimum. The reality however, is that this higher-than-average compensation has become the only factor keeping attrition in check. Many are now leaving for less money in the pursuit of real job satisfaction. This will likely continue until and unless "The Company" makes a real and lasting shift between the two – obedience & empowerment.

Retail is a very simple business – you trade merchandise for money. It should be expected that one could move between retail organizations with relative ease due to the similar nature of this business. This is generally true among retailers except this is not in the case of "The Company". "The Company" has created systems, processes and procedures that are so unnecessarily complex that new comers to "The Company" from other retail companies have a great deal of difficulty trying to adapt. With very few exceptions, they do not last _if_ they have worked in other retail previously. They simply find it too complicated – too incredibly complex. However, if they come from an industry outside of retail, they have a much better chance. The reason for the lower turnover when there is no previous retail experience is because they do not know any other way and just assume that this is how retail is done – up there in the ranks of complexity like rocket science and neurology. It is not any easier for them but out of ignorance, they apply themselves to learn it because they do not know any different. As mentioned above, if "The Company" does not make the shift and begins to experience massive turnover, they will be in serious trouble.

The most vivid example that I can use to illustrate the problem of over-complication in this organization is the process of ordering merchandise for sale to customers. Once again, the issue of "in-stock" comes up, but this example illustrates the problems encountered in trying to solve it. For much of the 15-year doom loop, no person in a store, including the store manager could order merchandise for his or her store. If the shelf was empty; if a customer wanted to purchase an unusually high quantity of goods; if a particular store sold a particular item in higher quantities than average; orders could not be placed to satisfy. The rules, restrictions and bureaucracy prevented anyone at store level from ordering anything. I think that it is only logical that if you are in the business to sell merchandise, it should be made relatively easy to obtain that merchandise to sell.

Only in the last few years has this been identified as a serious problem which I think in itself speaks volumes of the leadership problem in "The Company" in that it took several years to hear the cries of the needs of the customer. Despite the identification of the issue, it is still so incredibly complicated to order merchandise due to systems, spreadsheets, rules, criteria and limits – that it [ordering specific merchandise for the needs of the local customer] is still not leveraged in any significant way. All these layers of red tape have been put into place due to a lack of trust. The leadership of the company does not have enough faith in those that directly serve the customer to make good decisions on ordering merchandise. Therefore, a massive amount of rules and restrictions were implemented, completely forgetting about the customer, in order to protect the organization from the possibility of someone ordering too much.

If a company has overcomplicated what they do so extensively that they can no longer do what they intend to do (in this case sell merchandise), it is only a manner to time before the consequences of this bureaucracy come to pass.

The problems identified in the paragraphs above in fact stem from a lack of trust that the leadership of this organization has blanketed over the entire team. The excessive communication illuminates the fear that everyone in the organization is completely incompetent. There is an inability to trust that anyone in the organization can make decisions on even the most basic of tasks. This lack of trust has so effectively blinded this organization that the "machine" - or bureaucratic plague of over-complication - has tied its own hands behind its back, causing it to become an irrelevant player in the marketplace.

Tell them what to do – not "how-to"

"Never tell people how to do things. Tell them what to do and they will surprise you with their ingenuity"
General George S. Patton

Direction and instruction is obviously necessary. We cannot conduct business without it, at least not with any sense of organization and common purpose. But how much is too much? Where do you draw the line? The answer lies in what you want at the end of the day. If you want staunch obedience - an organization that does not think and does only and everything that you tell them – overburden it with instruction as outlined above using "The Company" as an example. However, if you want an organization that is empowered to think and make decisions for themselves - an organization that is entrepreneurial and one that develops and pioneers leading edge products, programs and services - you will need to limit and shape your communication appropriately. It has become clear to me that you cannot have it both ways.

I hope I have illustrated clearly what happens when you continuously bombard with instruction and "how-to", using "The Company" as the example. The majority of people want to contribute, have responsibility and be provided with room to develop and experiment with their own ideas. This provides fulfillment and purpose, which is the most important factor in any person's job satisfaction. If an individual finds fulfillment and purpose in what they do, all the other factors such as compensation, hours of work, location, etc. become secondary. People will work for less money if they can find fulfillment in what they do. On the other hand, without job fulfillment and purpose, it matters little how superior your pay, benefits and working conditions are – you will likely eventually lose that person. I have found that the more responsibility that you extend to an individual, the more that they will be willing to take, which results in increased job satisfaction. There are of course exceptions to everything, and not everyone wants increased responsibility. I would suggest that these individuals are not, or should not be those that are in a position of leadership. In any case, it is impossible to increase a person's level of responsibility if you always tell them both what to do and how to do it.

Direction, instruction and "how-to" should never exceed that which is absolutely necessary. This means it should only be what those in your organization would not, or could not know. I suggest that direction would fall into two distinct categories, strategic and technical. For the sake of clarity, here is how I would describe these two categories:

Strategic

This is information that is more visionary and conceptual in nature. It gives guidance to the organization on how to plan and provides framework for decision-making. For example, a software company's strategic direction to improve the support they provide on their product after the sale should cause the following types of changes to occur:

- Finance division to provide a higher working budget for the after-sale support team.
- It should cause the support group to solicit feedback from the sales team in order to provide support that is more effective.

- It should prompt the marketing division to put more emphasis on the after-sale support than it had in the past.

Essentially, every person in the organization would have this new strategic direction of improving after-sale service in mind and incorporate it into their planning and decision-making.

Technical

Technical information and instruction is very specific in nature. It informs the organization of new product, specifications and details that must be known in order to effectively provide the service or product for which the organization exists. For example, a restaurant chain provides specifics for ingredients and amounts in its various recipes.

There needs to be a limit on the information provided. Communication should never be designed to cover that which should be known. This temptation (to over-communicate) will increase more and more as an organization grows. It is harmful to continue to review and go over old information or "learnings" because someone may have missed or forgotten it. That information should definitely be available for reference, but avoid the temptation to re-broadcast whenever someone slips up.

Strategic information should always be directional. In the example provided above, if the software company communicated the strategic direction and then proceeded to advise every division how it affects them and how to bring that strategy to life in their area; good thinking, initiative and entrepreneurship would be suppressed. The same thing happens when the technical details go beyond what is necessary. For example, communicating to a store manager, instructions on how to unlock the front doors would be both excessive and unnecessary. This type and level of over-communication in both cases – strategic and technical - puts the intelligence of the recipient or audience into question. It is often done by well meaning people with good intentions but can be extremely damaging if a leader does not quickly intervene and stop it. If it is the leader that is generating this excessive and stifling communication, the leader needs to make a change within him or her self, or the leader will need to be changed.

To further emphasize the need for information to be streamlined, I will add that communication should often be less than required. Leave out some details in your communication that are not critical. Give your organization an opportunity to fill in some of the blanks themselves. This will help to create an open environment that encourages creativity and challenges everyone to think for him or herself, which will ultimately provide job satisfaction, fulfillment and reduced or even non-existent turnover.

Subsequently, leaders should spend their time observing and probing to gauge the level of understanding among their teams. It is likely that the creativity and new ideas that are generated from this approach of allowing your people to gain their own understanding rather than continually spoon feeding them will be pleasantly surprising.

ADJUSTING THE LEVEL OF COMMUNICATION

Everybody gets so much information all day long that they lose their common sense.
Gertrude Stein (1874 - 1946)

I have heard the following advice given to protect your hearing for life:

When listening to any type of audio – music, television, etc. – do the following to ensure that the volume is at a level that is sufficient for you to hear but not loud enough to cause hearing damage. Turn the volume level down until it is completely muted, then slowly turn the volume back up until it is at a comfortable level.

Try this the next time you are listening to the radio while driving in your car – it really does work. I find that I end up with a volume level that is much lower than when I started every time that I do this. I offer this up as an analogy for what an organization needs to do on a regular basis to ensure that the level of communication and complication has not become higher than what the recipients can receive without hearing damage – or damage to their ability to perform. Examine all "how-to", direction and instruction that your company is providing. Do this by asking those for whom it is intended. However, be careful of "yes people". You need to ask the right people – those that will give you honest answers. You will ultimately get true feedback if you first inform those that you are asking the reasons for your inquiry – that you are interested in curtailing excessive communication – that you desire to create an organization of creativity and good thinking. Challenge your organization to make the communication as tight as possible – the shorter and to the point – the better. Create "stop communicating" lists. In other words; lists of subjects, topics, formats and vehicles that you will stop communicating on due to their lack of any real value.

Besides the noble art of getting things done, there is the noble art of leaving things undone. The wisdom of life consists in the elimination of non-essentials.
Lin Yutang

Sometimes it is beneficial to completely throw out a method of communication or instruction and start again from scratch. If you re-create what you had before, it may be a sign that what you had was good, (be careful it could also be a sign of a lack of good thinking.) Chances are that the newly created communication method or vehicle will have changed to some degree – from a small amount to a completely different concept. Your new method would likely include changes in time, technology, and be adjusted according to the "learnings" acquired using the old method. Sometimes it is best to wipe the slate clean and start over – turn the volume off completely and then re-adjust it slowly upwards until it is just at the comfortable level.

You might be saying, "Everyone in my organization wants more communication – not less.". I have heard the same throughout my career. However, I have also found that it is not more communication that they are seeking, but better communication. More is not necessarily better. They are looking for concise, to the point, relevant and useful communication. In "The Company", this could have been accomplished at a level that was around 90% less than what is was being broadcasted. The other problem that you may come across is those people who actually desire detailed communication. If your organization has been subjected to over-communication for a long period of time, it may have created those individuals who want and must have detailed and explicit communication. These people have been conformed to the status of "doers". People will turn off their thinking capabilities if encouraged long enough. The good news is that they can also turn it back on. You will need to create a vacuum in the instruction and "how-to" for a period of time. Just as it took time for them to stop thinking, it will take time for them to start thinking again.

EMAIL ABUSE

What was once an amazing advance in communication, "email", is now a ball and chain for millions around the world. Many are slaves to their email; having to check and respond to hundreds of messages every day, and the advance of wireless technology increases its availability to 24 hours a day. Email makes it possible to send messages instantly anywhere in the world, which was almost unimaginable only 25 years ago. Unfortunately too much of a good thing can make you sick, and I think most will agree that the use of email is now at the point of abuse.

If we go back to the time before email or the fax machine was available, the method in which information was communicated was on paper – usually mailed or hand delivered. In order to control email and stop the abuse, I would suggest that email within an organization only be used as a replacement for the former "inter-office memo". This was the handwritten memo used to communicate back and forth between various entities within an organization. It was short and to the point. Email should be restricted to that purpose alone – simple, short and concise communication. This would mean that the ability to send an attachment within an email should be eliminated or at least restricted.

Email has encouraged poor planning and "last minuteness". Since an email can be created and sent in less than a minute and received on the other end in seconds; there is really no need to plan ahead, is there? Murphy's Law states that the work will expand to the time allotted hence most planning seems to take right up to the last minute to become complete. Email has afforded everyone with a little later "last minute" than we had 10 plus years ago. Before the advance of email, if it were not planned ahead of time, it would not get done. There was no way to communicate it if you missed the deadline, and to send an amendment to correct a poorly put together communication would be just as impossible.

Today, it seems that everything is left to the last minute. If companies were to recreate an environment that did not allow major plans, documents and manuals to be instantly transmitted, I believe that more thought and care would go into planning which of course would cause those plans to become much more effective. Spreadsheets, documents, manuals etc., should certainly be available electronically but in order to prevent the "last minuteness" previously mentioned, I do not believe that there should be any option to send via email.

The old "inter-office memos" were also difficult to

duplicate. To make multiple copies one could use carbon paper or it could be photocopied, but there was an increase in work for every extra copy sent out. For the benefit of the younger generation, carbon paper was a dark coloured sheet of paper with transferable ink. When placed between two sheets of paper it would allow that which is written on the top page to be transferred to the bottom page or pages depending on how many layers you built (and how hard you pushed on the pen). However, you still had to either stuff in an envelope or hand deliver each one. For this reason, these were copied very selectively and only on a strictly need to know basis. The "cc" on your email represents the words "carbon copy" and represents those who you send copies of your email for their reference. With the push of a button, email can be sent to an unlimited number of people. More often than not, since it is so easy, emails are sent to many more people than required. Organizations really need to calculate the time taken for each of the recipients to read and understand the email, respond to it, the time for the response to be read and understood, etc., and attach a dollar value to that time. Perhaps the number of emails sent, the average length of each email, and the average number of recipients copied should be one of those metrics that an organization measures. If an organization were to see the payroll dollars that are consumed in the creation and review of email alone – changes would most certainly be made. Once again, modeled after that old method of "inter-office memos", email should be restricted in number, size and only copied to relevant individuals - never to groups or send lists.

From my experience, the overuse of email is another one of the leading causes of frustration and reduced productivity in both organizations and among individuals privately. Consider the innumerable jokes, stories, and spam-type of emails that are bounced back and forth at the speed of light and the amount of time collectively that is consumed reading and filtering through them. Is anyone really better off after exposure to these? Perhaps one in a hundred, or even one in a thousand provides you with some information that makes you wiser. Sadly, it is not much different in organizations. Email in organizations is very much like the "soap" programs on television where in watching just one episode per month you can catch up on every story line that is playing out. In the company that I worked for, one could become informed enough to be effective in their job by reading only one days worth of email per week while simply deleting all the rest.

I had one eye opening experience with email because of an extended vacation. My vacation was at a location where email was not available, and I was away for almost three weeks. I advised my assistant, who had complete access to my email, to read my email each day deleting those, which were not important. My instructions were that by the time I returned there could only be a maximum of 20 email messages for me to read – the 20 that she felt were the most important. It is important to understand that the flow to my email inbox was between 70 and 100 per day. In three weeks that would amount to between 1,500 and 2,100 emails – she had to narrow it down to the 20 most important. Other than that, there was no further instruction on what I deemed to be more or less important – I left that decision up to her. When I returned, she had carried out what I had asked and had kept the number of email for me to review very close to 20 messages. Reading only that very small sampling of email, I was able to catch up very quickly with the current priorities and events. In fact, I probably could have been sufficiently informed with only 10 of them. Nothing broke down. The world did not stop spinning. No one died. In fact, it was one of the easiest "back-into-work-from-a-vacation-transitions" that I had ever experienced.

A NOTE ABOUT POWERPOINT®

Microsoft PowerPoint® is an excellent software program that helps one to build visual aids in order to provide support in conducting a presentation. When used effectively, PowerPoint® can make a good presentation great. However, it can be overused and abused as well. I have witnessed a culture that encourages presenters to compete with each other in the number of slides in their PowerPoint® presentations. The presenter with the most slides wins, encouraging a continual increase in the length of presentations. In "The Company" the more sophistication and detail in your slides – the smarter you are. In fact, without a PowerPoint® presentation, you are not considered a worthy presenter in "The Company". Whatever happened to an individual standing at the front of the room, presenting their subject matter without something on the screen behind them?

The truth is that the prevalent over-use of PowerPoint® is often used to mask the insecurity and lack of confidence of the presenting speaker. If you have something on the screen behind you, the audience will be looking at it – not at you. In addition, detailed and complicated slides imply increased intelligence in the presenter. People with low self-confidence utilize large and detailed PowerPoint® presentations in an attempt to try to mask that lack of confidence. Those that have a high degree of self-confidence and/or have something real and tangible to say, typically do not use PowerPoint® at all, or if they do use it, have only a few simple slides. If a presenter must rely entirely on a PowerPoint® presentation to relay their message we need to ask; do they really know and understand the message themselves? PowerPoint® supports and helps to streamline the presentation of those that have a message. When used properly it seamlessly integrates with the presenter and helps thoroughly communicate a point of view.

The following are guidelines that I would suggest for any organization:

Encourage presenters to do without

- Both self-confidence and presentation skills are increased when one can stand in front of a group and present effectively with no visual aids. This increased skill level will provide benefit to all areas of your organization.

- Presentations will become shorter and more to the point. Everyone's time will be used more effectively.

If used keep as short as possible

- If the presentation can be done on one page – resist the temptation to use more. Should be bullet points only – use as few words as possible.

Never read from a slide

- A presenter should always be looking at their audience when presenting.

The point of all communication is to convey a message, establish understanding and then make a request or urge the audience to take action. If one side – the presenter - is doing 100% of the talking there is no way to ensure that the audience has understood the message. A better approach would be to express the message or subject matter in the least words and time possible and then allow for questions from your audience to establish understanding. In my opinion, there is no substitute for a good discussion in establishing understanding.

DETAILS ARE IMPORTANT - BUT THERE IS AN ORDER

There is value in putting first things first. Imagine the teenager that purchases his or her first car. It is a used car and requires some work. The young person spends hours, days, weeks and months preparing that car for the road. He meticulously scrubs the interior. Sands and paints the entire exterior. New tires are purchased to replace the old worn and cracked ones. He replaces the brake pads and shoes. He changes the oil and fills the tank up with fuel. However, when he goes to start it he discovers that engine is in serious need of repair. Since he has spent all of his time and money on repairs of lesser importance, he is unable to use that car.

There is an order in how needs are to be met. Dr. Abraham Maslow, a 20th century behaviour scientist and psychologist identified the basic needs common to all people and cultures and arranged them according to priority in the "hierarchy of needs"[2]:

1. Physiological (health, food, sleep)

2. Safety (shelter, removal from danger)
3. Belonging (love, affection, being part of groups)
4. Esteem (self-esteem and esteem from others)
5. Self actualization (achieving individual potential)

In order of priority means that the first need is always met before the second, the second before the third, and so on. When a health crisis hits an individual, little else matters until they recover from it. Of course, significance would be the last thing on the mind of an individual who was without food and water for any length of time - that person would most likely perish in the process of trying to obtain significance. Understanding on what an individual is currently focused in this hierarchy of needs is vital to ensure you are addressing and assisting them in the most relevant manner.

Needs or tasks in a business or organization also need to be addressed in order of priority and a violation of this order will have negative consequences. For example, it would be ridiculous for a new airline company to purchase aviation fuel prior to the procurement of the airplanes themselves.

Every business and organization has those issues that are the basics for their purpose. For a homebuilder it is a constant demand for new homes and real estate on which to build them. For a retail company, it is getting the goods to sell in a timely manner. It would make no sense for the homebuilder to purchase lumber without contracts to build homes or for the retailer to send out advertisements to customers to come in to purchase without first ensuring that merchandise is available. There is an order and priority for the fundamental functions of any organization to be carried out.

Increased technology and over complication of processes and systems have a way of causing organizations to lose sight of these "basics". Organizations would be wise to specifically list their own hierarchy of needs – their own priority list and follow it relentlessly. The leadership should not allow the organization to move beyond any point on the list of needs until the previous need has been met. In addition, regular visits to the list should be conducted to ensure that none of the initial needs have been neglected. Just as an individual always keeps their eye on their food, clothing and shelter while working down the list, so should any organization keep their eye on the top of their list to ensure nothing is forgotten or neglected.

Occam's razor is a principle attributed to the 14th-century English logician and Franciscan friar William of Ockham[3]. It is often paraphrased as "All other things being equal, the simplest solution is the best." It has also been cited in the following ways:

"If you have two equally likely solutions to a problem, pick the simplest"

"Everything should be made as simple as possible, but not simpler"

"One should not increase, beyond what is necessary, the number of entities required to

explain anything"

Businesses and organizations should pursue the goal of making everything as simple as possible to understand, operate, execute and duplicate within them. In my opinion there are two reasons behind the over-complication and sophistication of systems, processes and procedures. The first and most prevalent is due to well-meaning people that do not want anyone to miss anything and try to compensate ahead of time. This problem is also relatively easy to change. The other - which is cultural and much more difficult to change - is an effort for some to make their positions and him or herself as a person, more important in order to justify their jobs and endeavour to make him or herself irreplaceable. The reality is that we are all replaceable. I once heard the following analogy to illustrate just how quickly any person in an organization will be replaced after they leave:

Stick your hand into a pail full of water. Pull it out. As quickly as the water rushes in to replace the area that your hand was in, is as quickly as you will be replaced when you leave an organization.

We all need to get over ourselves and start to do what is right for the organization and everyone in it. This is the best way to add value to yourself and to the company for which you work. Adding value to your company is the best way to justify your job – not by complicating that which you do.

Security is mostly a superstition. It does not exist in nature, nor do the children of men as a whole experience it. Avoiding danger is no safer in the long run than outright exposure. Life is either a daring adventure or nothing.
Helen Keller

This entire subject of simplification links back to focus and clarity. If everyone in an organization maintains his or her focus on that purpose for which the organization exists – there will be less over-complication. The idea is to meet the goals of the company – not to build complicated systems, processes and communication. If people within your organization cannot understand the systems that are employed, and the very ones that designed them cannot explain those systems; the systems are too complicated. I have always used the following to test my own personal understanding; if I cannot explain it to anyone, in terms and language that they understand, then I really do not understand it myself.

For the same reason that the theory of communism failed, a business that seeks to download and dictate every instruction and detail will achieve only minimal success and will certainly not stand the test of time. The greatest flaw of communism is that instead of inspiring dreams, aspirations and creativity in individuals, it suppressed them. If organizations do not seek to tap into the ideas, insights, creativity, imagination and personal drive of those that they employ, they will surely limit their potential and longevity.

Strong leaders seek to simplify. Good leaders understand that tapping into their most important resource – the minds of the people that work for them – will make them and their organization infinitely more successful. They trust the people they hired to make decisions and take calculated risks on behalf of the company that they lead. They intuitively understand the link between that trust and job satisfaction.

*The deepest craving of human nature
is the need to be appreciated.*

William James

Chapter Eight

RECOGNITION

"THE COMPANY"

The subject of "recognition" is not an issue that is specific to companies and organizations, but applies to every relationship in life. Recognition cannot be mandated or enforced. It is a leadership issue, and with all leadership issues it can, and must be modeled in order to make it part of any culture. In any organization, you will find both leaders that excel at it and those at the other end of the spectrum. Its prevalence or absence varies from organization to organization, work group to work group and person to person in the same degree that personalities differ from one another. Any attempt to try to increase recognition in an organization beyond leading it by example from within, will lead to disingenuous and artificial resource consuming efforts.

On more than one occasion, "The Company" attempted

to increase recognition through a program or system. The programs fell under various names over the course of time but were always generally the same in structure. They [the programs] included a type of certificate or piece of paper, which was known or understood to represent a gesture of appreciation. The form would be filled out by anyone and then be presented to any other person in "The Company" at any level to represent his or her appreciation for something that had been done or accomplished. The concept at its core was a good idea and certainly encouraged and reminded everyone to take time to provide a "thank you" to others around them. The demise of each of these programs began when the company did what it does so well – it decided to track and measure it. That tracking hinged on these questions:

- How many appreciatory comments this week in the workgroup, the store or the division?
- How do those amounts compare with the other workgroups, stores or divisions?

Once you start to compare, the competition begins. Subsequently, awards were designed to recognize each work group with the highest amounts of recorded recognition, in other words it was – recognizing recognition. Competing on something like the number of times you recognized someone is like having a competition around how many times you tell your spouse that you love him or her. Does it really mean anything anymore? The recognition itself became insincere, fake and obviously inflated for the sake of getting personal recognition on how many times you recognized others. You may have to read the previous sentence a few times to understand what was going on. This is a great example of what happens when you spend too much time down in the weeds failing to look at the big picture. Obviously, none of these programs ever lasted and did little to nothing to improve the propensity for "The Company" to recognize great effort and results.

Respect

I can ride the wave of a great compliment on something that I have done for weeks and in some cases, months. However, when someone compliments a characteristic of my personality – I never forget it. One of the most uplifting things in life is to receive a positive comment about a personality trait, especially if it is something that you personally have never really identified in yourself. These are character-shaping moments. The interesting thing about these character-shaping comments is that I also never forget the person who provided them. My level of respect reaches new heights for every person that provides me with a nice or positive comment about my personality. I will do almost anything for them. I become a fan of theirs – an advocate, standing behind them in support in any circumstance regardless of their relationship – boss, friend or acquaintance. As leaders, isn't it this that we are looking for from those that report to us - loyalty, support, respect? And since this is what we desire from those that report to us, it makes sense that our supervisors would hope to obtain those same qualities in us.

The attributes of respect, support and loyalty do not come with title - they must be earned. I have never struggled with this concept – it always made logical sense to me. I thank my parents for instilling this in me. Nevertheless, I am continuously amazed at how many people in this world feel that they deserve respect because of the job title, or rank that they hold. They seem to feel that regardless of how they have treated others, they should command immediate and devoted respect, and become genuinely disturbed and put off when they do not receive it.

Outside of the obvious boss to employee relationship, let me provide an example that I encounter on a regular basis. When you work with the public, which every organization must do in some way, shape or form, you will always encounter individuals that have a need, want a favour, a special discount or possibly want to express a complaint. Most people make their request on the merit of the request itself – who they are, is not the issue and has no relevance to the situation. However, there are a certain percentage of people in these circumstances (thankfully the minority) that will state their title or credentials first – before their case or request. It could be in the form of handing you a business card. It may be the opening paragraph of a letter or it could be simply verbal. I am not talking about situations where their title is in fact relevant. For example: if it is the Fire Marshal and an exit door is blocked – the title of the person in this case is important and provides a needed sense of urgency to their request. But what does the fact that a person has a personalized business card, special designation or title have to do with a complaint on the service they received. Is it that everyone ought to know that they are someone special and should never be treated a certain way? Is it that due to their status they should receive special treatment? These are the people who believe respect simply comes hand in hand with title – as a gift or a right. More often than not, I find my assumptions confirmed -that they will not be extending any personal respect or courtesy toward me because it is not within them to give.

These are people who want something and feel that they should have it just because of who they are. In life this may get you somewhere for a time, but will eventually catch up with you and bring with it consequences of mediocrity, limited potential and failure.

I once heard it said, "One of the best ways to see a person's true character is to observe how they treat those people around them, in particular, those that can't do anything for them."

We truly do reap what we sow. If you sow seeds of respect, you will reap respect in return. In other words, if you extend respect to others, you will receive respect back from others in return, and in relation to the amount you have given out. Respect every human being that you come into contact with and treat them how you would like to be treated - you will get the reward of respect back in abundance. This is both a principle and a law, and therefore a guarantee.

WHAT EXACTLY IS RECOGNITION?

What do we like to talk about above any other subject? Ourselves. Most of us can talk for hours about anything to do with us - our experiences, family, circumstances etc. We all strive to be noticed and to be important. The drive to be famous for many human beings on this planet is insatiable.

Recognition is the observation and acknowledgment of good effort, positive results and superior strengths.

To recognize is to notice others, notice the accomplishments of others and notice the personal characteristics and strengths in others. We all want others to see the good work that we are doing, to be aware of our efforts and accomplishments. It is not enough to just observe, but a positive remark or comment must be made on that observation in order to complete the recognition.

When recognition is provided effectively, the recipient should feel some or all of the following:

- He/she understands how hard I have worked at this.
- He/she is grateful for the accomplishments/results I have achieved.
- He/she believes that I have unique and special knowledge or abilities.
- He/she is pleased with what I am doing.
- He/she is happy with me.
- He/she believes in me.

Recognition is most meaningful one on one – person to person. Certainly, groups can and should be recognized, but group recognition is spread across a large number of people and therefore watered down. When you identify and remark on issues, efforts and accomplishments on an individual basis, you exponentially elevate that person's job satisfaction and morale. While it certainly is appropriate at times and in certain circumstances to recognize individual strengths in a group setting, you may end up building animosity if you do it continually and has the potential to erode the group's morale. The best definition of morale that I have heard is, "faith in the leader at the top".[1] That faith will come with respect, and respect is earned through good leadership, which is impossible without recognizing the efforts, accomplishments and strengths of your people.

I have encountered my fair share of leaders that treat everyone below them as if they are machines. They drive them like many farmers use machinery. There is no relationship required between the man and machine. The machine is made to work hard continuously and never requires rest. Other than fuel (pay) and the occasional oil change (benefits), they should require nothing else. If they ever break down, after they have the wrench thrown at them, they are sent away to get fixed – and - it is imperative that they are fixed quickly. I am sure that you have met these types over time. Here are some identifiers:

- They only call when they need something.
- They ask how you are doing – but it becomes abundantly clear that they really do not want to know. I.e.: They ask, "How are you doing?" Then while you are explaining that there was a death in your family, they make it obvious that they are not listening by cutting you off with "good to hear" and then state their request.
- They do not really care about your problems nor do they want to hear about them – they tell you to "fix them".
- Some cannot even remember your name – they know you by your title I.e.: what you do (combine, tractor etc.)

The good news is that life takes care of these types of leaders. There is a ceiling to the success that people who treat others in this manner, will ever achieve. More often than not, that ceiling will in time come crashing down on them. They will never accomplish any lasting success. It comes back to the principle of sowing and reaping. They will eventually harvest the seeds that they have sown and one cannot obtain a good harvest from sowing seeds of disrespect and contempt.

Good leaders care about those they work with. They do not consider those they work with as working under them, but rather with them. That mindset, which comes from an attitude of respect, changes how they interact and treat everyone around them. It comes from within and is genuine and sincere. They understand that the more they can push others up, the better and more successful they themselves become.

I have seen these five attributes in great leaders around the subject of recognition:

1) Know them as a person first

Good leaders take time to get to know their people. They seek to learn about their family, where they grew up, their hobbies, and personal interests, etc. They ask questions and listen carefully with a heartfelt desire to truly learn what gives them life outside of work.

2) Understand their dreams, values and aspirations

Caring leaders find out the dreams, plans and aspirations of their people. They unselfishly do everything within their power to help them achieve those dreams. They seek to find out what is important to them – their values. They understand that they will achieve immeasurably more success by helping as many others as possible to become successful.

3) *Understand their strengths and weaknesses*

Good leaders take the time to identify both the strengths (what they do well) and the weakness (what they do not do as well) in their people. They do not try to fix their weaknesses, but rather focus on strengthening the strengths. They understand that their people can be exponentially more successful by working on their strengths.

4) *Appreciate & Acknowledge*

Good leaders know and understand the challenges of their team, and because they know; they truly appreciate what they are up against. This awareness brings both empathy and understanding. When our leaders know what we are up against and are working on; and they make that awareness and understanding evident by their actions and support, our morale is high regardless of the challenge. The level of our loyalty, support and respect for that leader is at its peak.

5) *Gratitude*

Since good leaders know us personally, and have taken the time to understand our challenges, they are in a unique position to express gratitude. They use honest sincere "thank-yous" to express that gratitude. Because these leaders are so close to what we are doing, those expressions of gratitude always seem to be in the right form, for the right thing, and at the right time. We are never in want at the "recognition well" of a great leader.

The above attributes have been numbered on purpose.

Leaders that exhibit these out of this order, or only exhibit some attributes and not others - are less effective. For example: A show of gratitude to an individual that you do not know is usually not effective. If a leader does not understand an individual's challenges, that gratitude may miss the mark and illuminate that leader's ignorance. The extension of gratitude in this case could do more harm than good.

It may seem hard to believe that the extension of gratitude can do more harm than good. In addition to the example provided in this paragraph, there are also those who throw out gratitude so excessively that their insincerity is palpable. Their duplicity is incredibly transparent. I find that I actually perceive any compliment provided by a person like this to be a criticism and sometimes a complaint. I look behind the compliments from these people and my intuition tells me that they only compliment that which they are envious of, or that which they dislike or do not appreciate. I take their compliments negatively because of the exaggerations.

Methods

The most effective form of recognition is a simple "Thank you", but in some circumstances that may not be enough. It may take monetary rewards, public recognition, special treatment or favours. The specifics of this vary from organization to organization and person to person, and provide a great opportunity to make your recognition original and personal. I would suggest that it always be appropriate for the situation – neither too large of too small. I.e.: a ten thousand dollar bonus for completing a small project ahead of time might be a little over the top, while a verbal thank you may not be enough for annual results that are double the company average. If your recognition has the result of making the individual feel as outlined in the identifiers mentioned previously, I would suggest that it has sufficiently reached the mark.

In the book "The Power of Focus", authors Jack Canfield, Mark Victor Hansen and Les Hewitt, suggest the use of handwritten thank you notes.[2] They advocate taking the time to write and send or hand-deliver personalized handwritten notes to express your appreciation and gratitude. The profound impact of receiving one of these personally has certainly convinced me that this approach is an excellent method to employ in pursuit of recognition.

I believe that whatever method one chooses to recognize will be perfect, if it is generated from a sincere desire to express gratitude and not from a motivation to manipulate.

⸻

When we hear the word recognition in a business environment, we think of the simple act of saying thank you. In the example of "The Company", those "thank-yous" were being generated artificially via the various programs that it implemented. Similar to any superficial or band-aid type of program that seeks to treat the symptoms rather than the roots of the issue; true change in the form of increased recognition, will never be realized by this approach.

A sincere expression of thanks on a regular basis is the

manifestation of recognition – the result that comes out of the genuine and caring leader. Attempts to provide it deceptively in a manner to gain favour and manipulate others is incredibly transparent and has the opposite effect in that it creates mistrust, and erodes loyalty and support. Recognition cannot be faked.

The leader that understands and cares for their people – that understands their people's challenges and problems – that takes the time and energy to individually express their appreciation and gratitude, reaps the benefits of sowing those seeds of recognition. The benefits are a bountiful harvest of; lower turnover and attrition, increased success in attracting new and talented employees, strong morale among their teams, less friction, more harmony, improved results and personal success.

In the end, this interest in individuals is the only way to obtain true respect, loyalty and support from those people with whom you work. Many do try to obtain it with artificial attempts at recognition, and as mentioned previously – anyone can see through it. These manipulative leaders become mystified by the success of those that genuinely understand and practice recognition. Recognition is more about character than anything else. It comes from within – it comes from the heart.

Are you a leader who provides character shaping comments and praise? Do you know your people well enough to be able to provide compliments on the work, results and personality of your people? I encourage you to try to put into practice the recommendations and principles within this chapter. I expect that you will personally witness how much of a positive affect that they will have on your work group or team.

I started this chapter with the statement that recognition applies to every relationship in life. This of course includes our friends and family. We do not usually link the word leadership to the relationships that we have outside of the work environment. The truth is that we lead in every area of life – good or bad – in a positive or negative manner. It is far more effective to invest time trying to find ways to compliment and push others up, rather than correcting or criticizing. Imagine the difference that approaching your relationship with your spouse, kids, parents, siblings, etc. from the framework of the five attributes described earlier. Imagine the positive effect of looking for all those things that they are doing right and then just mentioning them instead of those things - in your opinion -that they are doing wrong. The law applies to all areas of life. The more time that you spend in helping others to become better, the better, you yourself will become.

What luck for rulers that men do not think.

Adolf Hitler (1889 - 1945)

Chapter Nine

THE FUTURE OF EFFECTIVE LEADERSHIP

Why have we created a world where sincerity and honesty are so hard to find? We have become accustomed to cautiously evaluate everything our politicians say to try to figure out what they mean, how they really feel, what they will really do. Why is that? It is likely because they do not actually say what they really mean but instead say what they think we want to hear, or better said, what will win them favour with the vast majority of voters in order to be elected to office. This is what is called "politics" and it plays out in all facets of life. We see it in businesses and organizations of any type or size. We see it in our relationships with friends, with our extended family and sometimes even within our closest family.

So why do we do it? Why do we spend so much time and energy crafting our communication to elicit certain desired responses? The honest answer is that we do it in order to manipulate. We do it to manipulate others to do, think or feel the way that we want them to feel. As hard as it is to accept, it is in reality, dishonest and deceptive. Just to be clear, I am not talking about courtesy and politeness within our communication, which is important and necessary. I am referring instead to the habit of saying other than what you really mean. For example, overwhelmingly praising an idea, program or system in front of the creator of that idea, program or system, in order to win favour with them. All of this, despite the fact that you may have some criticism that would prove to be helpful in improving that persons creation, or, you feel that their creation is either useless or close to useless.

Perhaps it is just a Canadian thing. We Canadians think of ourselves as decidedly polite and never want to do anything that could offend another. But no, I see the same thing in the United States as well. The fear of offending someone else or "political correctness" as it has come to be known, has grown so much that it has begun to affect our ability to productively function as a society. In the same way, it has reduced the productivity and effectiveness of many organizations.

Democracy consists of choosing your dictators, after they've told you what you think it is you want to hear.
Alan Corenk

Regardless of my opinion on the subject, it would seem that if you are to be successful in today's business world, you must conform and become "political". People generally have adverse reactions when someone tells it like it is or how they really feel. Politicians face intense persecution if they share an opinion that is unpopular or "politically incorrect". More often than not, their comments prove to be career ending. I suppose that if you want to become an elected member of government, you really have no choice but to play this game of appeasement. There certainly are examples of men and women that have successfully risen above this mould of "political correctness" and have told it like it was - how they really felt. However, these are typically within the lower levels of government and would experience trouble if they were to attempt to springboard up to any significant national or lead position. Most organizations and companies mirror the political world in their own version of "political correctness". But should it be this way? Should the ability to deceive and manipulate be a prerequisite to success in either the business or political worlds?

Personally, I do not think that "playing politics" or "being political" is healthy or constructive but instead is destructive. I believe that we need to change and reverse this negative trend. I believe that we need leaders to bring sincerity and honesty back to all facets of society and business. I have shared throughout this book the negative consequences that result in a company from the lack of honesty, excessive bureaucracy and political posturing. The benefits would be unimaginable if we could shift the energy from these unhelpful activities and behaviours to honesty and sincerity – in other words – telling it like it is and how we really feel.

In the book, "The Success Principles" by Jack Canfield and Janet Switzer; a universal life principle is shared: *"How you do anything is how you do everything."*[1] Allow me to link this life principle to the focus of the book you are now reading. When I exhibit excellence in my work, I most likely exhibit excellence in everything that I do. If I act with integrity in my business dealings, I am likely to act with integrity in everything I do. However, if I am duplicitous in my communication, am I duplicitous in everything? The principle works both ways - positive and negative - and the answer is "yes"! We have certainly seen examples in the news over the past few years of the end result of duplicity and deception in the business world with a number of the top executives ending up in prison. The impact on the lives of those linked and associated to companies such as Enron and WorldCom in the U.S. could never be overstated. This game of "political correctness" - with its manipulation and deceit - can often lead to devastating outcomes leaving many casualties in its wake.

Throughout this book, I have outlined the problems and the pitfalls of "The Company" which have prevented it from achieving maximum success, or, depending on how you define success – any success at all. You may have found the stories and examples highly critical. However, I am simply telling it like it is. I obviously did not sugar-coat anything. I chose to be completely and brutally honest - to face the facts as they are. So, does my approach make them any worse than they are? No, the problems of "The Company" are both real and limiting.

What if I had explained the problems of "The Company" less critically, with some political spin to try to minimize how ineffective the "The Company" really is? What if I had chosen to pick out only the positive things that "The Company" was doing and then followed up each chapter with what I think it could improve upon? What if I did not tell it like it is – if I was not completely honest? In other words, what if I wrote this book from the mould that "The Company" and many organizations work within? If I had chosen that route, there would be no lesson - no identification of leadership principles and nothing that one could take away and utilize in their own life or business. Essentially, there would not be a book.

As I have argued in this book, we cannot make change until we have faced the truth – however hard that truth is to face. The fact that I could not write a book without stating the brutally honest truth is the same reason that "The Company" cannot find success. Refusing to acknowledge, recognize and admit realities and problems do not make them go away. This denial also inhibits any action against those problems. We do not work to fix things that are not broken.

When we do admit that things are not working as well as they could be, we start to see a contrast or a gap between good and not so good. Contrast brings clarity. It is much easier to distinguish the darkness of a shade of black when compared to the colour white than to the colour grey, dark blue or green. The contrast reveals the truth, and the greater the contrast the more effectively the truth is illuminated. When we see our problems and shortfalls with maximum intensity, we truly see how far away we are from where we should be.

The sad reality is that political posturing and bureaucratic games outlined throughout this book are not exclusive to "The Company". They are played out in varying degrees in almost every company and organization. As you read through the following chapter summaries, identify which apply to the organization that you currently work in or lead.

Chapter 2:

Focus and Clarity – forgetting that purpose or reason for which you exist - wandering aimlessly chasing any and every opportunity that pops up.

Chapter 3:

Listening and Leading – leaders that think they know all and know best for everyone.

Chapter 4:

Customer Focused – subscribing to the rhetoric that our company is focused on the customer but not walking the talk.

Chapter 5:

Don't let the "accountants" take over – allowing the "number lovers" to run the organization and make every decision based on a number without consulting with reality.

Chapter 6:

You are only as good as your weakest link – assuming that the organization is well fortified in every area.

Chapter 7:

Simplify – overwhelming and crippling instruction, direction and bureaucracy.

Chapter 8:

Recognition – the absence of gratitude or acknowledgement of efforts of the team.

The preceding summaries were of course stated from a negative standpoint. I would submit and venture to guess that there is a correlation between the current success of your organization and the extent that it matches the seven themes. If you find difficulty matching any of these themes to your company – my hunch is, that success is coming with relative ease. However, if you felt that they described your organization to a tee, my guess is that your organization is likely in financial turmoil and struggling to achieve any positive success.

This book and the principles within are not based on detailed research or complicated science. I do not claim to be a brilliant academic. I have personally witnessed many who have entered an occupation with the book smarts of school and hit the wall of real life and practicality. The two do not always mesh. Life and experience are infinitely better teachers than the textbooks of education and there are some things that cannot be taught but must be acquired through experience.

Natural ability without education has more often attained to glory and virtue than education without natural ability.
Cicero (106 BC - 43 BC)

The lessons in this book are from personal experience and observation. They are the culmination of what does work and what does not work in real life and business. I hope that you have found them intuitive and not overly complicated. Complication helps no one. Simplification can sometimes be deceptive causing us to question, "Is it really that easy?" More often than not – it is.

Leadership is more about honesty and sincerity than anything else, which comes out of a genuine attitude of humility. This view contrasts with the prevailing model of the leader, which is one of authority, power, supremacy and dominance, or the leader that is larger than life to whom everyone is attracted.

A prerequisite for strong leadership is the ability to follow. The ability to follow provides one with the wisdom and knowledge of what it takes to cause others to follow them. One cannot effectively lead if he or she cannot effectively follow. There is a reason why no military would promote a soldier to a higher rank – a position of leadership – if one could not first demonstrate the ability to follow orders and instructions. Why would we think that it would be any different in the business world? Poor leadership in the military could cost lives and freedoms. Poor leadership in the business world could cause financial disaster. Entire nations can be destroyed by poor leadership in the political arena.

In summary, the leader who displays humility, sincerity and honesty, who works with others (alongside rather than over), with focused determination to realize a compelling and well communicated vision, is a leader who will achieve the most success in business and in life. This is the type of leader I want to follow. This is the kind of leader I want to become.

Here is a hypothetical story about the kind of leadership we really need to see in companies, organizations, the political arena and in the family.

Imagine a vice president in the boardroom of a struggling large organization, having to once again; explain why results are not meeting expectations. This setting has replayed itself repeatedly over the past several years with the company's declining profits. However, today is different. Rather than conforming to the usual political rhetoric and reciting a handful of the usual excuses from the company's own unwritten "List of excuses for poor results handbook", this executive decides to do something different. This decision is the result of a long period of reflection and observation into the reality of her organization. It comes from a purpose-filled desire to get honest with one's self and take an honest unfiltered look around her. This vice president decides to get real. It is a risk – an incredible risk. No one has ever done this. While she has figured out that the norm – the status quo – being political and deceptive has done nothing to change the results, she is not sure that anyone in the organization is ready for reality – ready for honesty, particularly the top leadership – the CEO. Never the less, she is tired of playing the game – being political and hiding her true feelings – the truth. It could cost her – it could get her fired. This is the reason that no one has done this before – fear – and it is fear, that has kept her from doing this… until today.

When it is her turn to stand and present her own poor results - which are no different from any of her peers – she reviews her numbers with an unfamiliar sense of brutal honesty that shocks everyone in the room. She reviews only the meaningful or consequential results – those that truly have an effect on the profitability of the company – both the good and the bad. She emphasizes the bad results in a way that conjures a sense of urgency to correct, forecasting what continued poor performance would do to the company. Her honest review of the results leave her peers feeling both relieved and embarrassed at the same time - a sense of relief that the attention is off of them and onto her, but also shame that they had not had the courage to present with such honesty. Despite their inner feelings, not one of them show any support and wait for the reaction of the CEO before they decide how they will respond.

There was now absolute silence as everyone waited to hear her explanations – what she was going to do about the numbers. This is what she said: "Today I could stand up here as I have so many times in the past and attempt to try to spin the numbers to make them sound better than they really are. I could try to divert your attention to some insignificant peripheral result that is positive to try to make my team and I look good. I could provide you with one of many excuses – all of which you have heard before - to try to justify the results. However, none of that will make any difference for the future. None of that will change and improve the results. It has not changed the results in the past and will not likely do so in the future. Therefore, today I am going to talk about what we really need to do to change our results – to climb out of the slide in profitability that we have been experiencing. The number one issue that we need to solve is...."

This vice president proceeds to tell the group what the organization needs to do to be successful again. She speaks with an honesty and sincerity that has not been heard before in this particular boardroom. She attacks the "sacred cows" of the organization. She speaks of all those issues that everyone knows are problems – hindrances – but are political suicide to criticize. She challenges the status quo of the organization as if she was an outside consultant with no bias or ties to the company. Then, because of her brutal honesty and the fact that the real issues are now out in the open, she is able to provide a number of possible strategies and solutions to the problems.

What happens next depends entirely on the CEO. The vice president's directness and honesty could be seen as a refreshing wakeup call to the organization. It could become the catalyst for a new direction that brings the organization back to successful results. On the other hand, it could be seen as negative and divisive and as a result, that vice president will most certainly be replaced. The outcome has cultural implications. If she is supported, a new wave of refreshing change away from political correctness will be the result. If she does not receive support, the culture of "don't think outside of the box" or "don't express how you really feel" will be dutifully reinforced.

Regardless of the outcome, this vice president is the leader that we should all aspire to become. She is prepared to take a personal risk for the benefit of the organization. She exhibited a great deal of courage. She decided to do the right thing rather than to continue to just do things right.

While this story is hypothetical, it reflects one of the main challenges of a leader in any setting. That is to have courage, stand behind your convictions, be honest, and do what your conscience is telling you to do.

Whether we are looking at a business, an organization of any kind, the political realm or personal relationships, the outcomes (results, products and effects) – positive or negative - can be linked back to the leadership applied in them. In other words:

ALL OUTCOMES ARE A CONSEQUENCE OF LEADERSHIP.

Do not be deceived: God cannot be mocked. A man reaps what he sows. (Galatians 6:7- NIV)

CONSEQUENCE OF LEADERSHIP

I leave you with two questions. If you do not completely agree with some or all of the principles outlined throughout this book, I would encourage you to ask yourself the following questions about your own beliefs on leadership and the principles that you employ:

How have they been working for you?

How has your leadership been working for your organization?

NOTES

Chapter 2: Focus & Clarity
[1] http://www.businessplans.org/mission.html

Chapter 3: Listening and Leading
[1] The Five Dysfunctions of a Team: A Leadership Fable
By Patrick M. Lencioni
Published by John Wiley & Sons, Incorporated, 2002
ISBN 0787962805, 9780787962807
240 pages

[2] Good To Great: Why Some Companies Make The Leap...and Others Don't
By Jim Collins, James C. Collins
Published by HarperCollins, 2005
ISBN 0066621003, 9780066621005
320 pages

[3] The World's Most Powerful Leadership Principle: How to Become a Servant Leader
By James C. Hunter
Published by Waterbrook Press, 2004
ISBN 1578569753, 9781578569755
224 pages

Chapter 4: Customer Focused
[1] http://www.competitionbureau.gc.ca/epic/site/cb-bc.nsf/en/01262e.html
[2] http://www.cacds.com/onrecord/documents/ScannerAccuracyAnnualR-eportV-FINAL2007.pdf
[3] http://en.wikipedia.org/wiki/Pareto_principle

Chapter 5: Don't let the "accountants" take over
[1] Built to Last: Successful Habits of Visionary Companies
By James Charles Collins, Jerry I. Porras, Jim Collins
Published by HarperBusiness Essentials, 2002
ISBN 0060516402, 9780060516406
368 pages

Chapter 6: You are only as good as your weakest link
[1] http://en.wikipedia.org/wiki/Space_Shuttle_Challenger_disaster
[2] http://www.marcusbuckingham.com/home.php

Chapter 7: Simplify
[1] widely circulated on internet under the title "Modern Day Parable" – author unknown
[2] http://changingminds.org/explanations/needs/maslow.htm
[3] http://en.wikipedia.org/wiki/Ockham_razor

Chapter 8: Recognition
[1] The 360 Degree Leader: Developing Your Influence from Anywhere in the Organization
By John C. Maxwell
Published by Nelson Business, 2006
ISBN 0785260927, 9780785260929
315 pages

[2] Authors: Jack Canfield, Mark Victor Hansen, Les Hewitt
Publication Date: March 2000
Publisher: Hci
ISBN-10: 1558747524
ISBN-13: 9781558747524

Chapter 9: The future of Effective Leadership
[1] Authors: Jack Canfield, Janet Switzer
Publication Date: January 2007
Publisher: Collins
ISBN-10: 0060594896
ISBN-13: 9780060594893

DIANA NYAD

THE PURSUIT OF THE IMPOSSIBLE